F. KAG

MONEY AND MAR

Also by Jan Pahl

PRIVATE VIOLENCE AND PUBLIC POLICY
A REFUGE FOR BATTERED WOMEN
MANAGERS AND THEIR WIVES (*with R. E. Pahl*)

Money and Marriage

Jan Pahl

Senior Research Fellow
University of Kent at Canterbury

MACMILLAN

First published 1989

Published by
MACMILLAN EDUCATION LTD
Houndmills, Basingstoke, Hampshire RG21 2XS
and London
Companies and representatives
throughout the world

Typeset by Latimer Trend & Company Ltd, Plymouth

Printed in the People's Republic of China

British Library Cataloguing in Publication Data
Pahl, Jan, *1937–*
Money and marriage
1. Great Britain. Marriage.
Financial aspects
I. Title
332.024
ISBN 0–333–38767–8 (hardcover)
ISBN 0–333–38768–6 (paperback)

For Kate, John and Nick, with love

Contents

List of tables and figures

Tables

Figures

Acknowledgements

This study was funded by the Economic and Social Research Council and by the Joseph Rowntree Memorial Trust. I am glad to have this opportunity to express my gratitude for their support.

I should also like to thank most warmly all those who did interviewing, data analysis, typing and word processing for the project. I very much appreciated the skill, energy and enthusiasm with which they worked. They included: Alison Allen, Jeremy Barton, Sian Calnan, Christine Elcombe, Frances Evans, Barbara Holland, Mary Knox, Helly Langley, Gill Rudge and Barbara Wall.

Many colleagues and friends have given generously of their time, support and knowledge. I should like to thank all those who have taken an interest in the study, and especially John Butler, Hugh Cunningham, Meredith Edwards, Hilary Land, Belinda Meteyard, David Morgan, Thea Sinclair and members of the Resources within Households Study Group. Lou Opit's help with data analysis and computing was invaluable: I thank him for his intellectual generosity. Ray Pahl and I have been pooling our money and our ideas for many years now and I am most grateful to him for all that he has contributed to the study.

Above all I am pleased to acknowledge my debt to the people who agreed to be interviewed, without whom the research could not have been done. When individuals are mentioned in the pages which follow, their names and some personal details have been altered in order to preserve the confidentiality of what they told us. I should like to thank most warmly all those who welcomed us into their homes and who trusted us with information about a very private aspect of their lives.

JAN PAHL

1

Introduction

The financial arrangements of married people must be one of the most private, yet also one of the most important of topics. The secrecy with which couples protect their financial affairs is as great as the secrecy surrounding sexual relationships; yet compared with the enormous literature, both academic and popular, on the subject of sex, little has been written on money in marriage. Knowing more about financial arrangements within marriage would increase our understanding of the nature of relationships between men and women, both in marriage and more generally. In contemporary society money is a medium of exchange, not only in the conventional economic sense, but also in a social and ideological sense. The fact that it is so very private is perhaps a testimony to its importance.

This study grew out of previous research concerned with violence against women within marriage (Pahl, 1985). Interviewing abused women at a refuge I found that many of them claimed to be financially better off since leaving their husbands. All were living on supplementary benefit (now, income support) receiving sums of money which represented the minimum amount on which anyone in Britain was expected to live. Yet on these meagre amounts they felt 'better off'. As I became sensitive to the implications of what the women were saying I started to ask about financial arrangements in the households from which they had come. It was clear that some of the husbands had had substantial incomes, but had kept so much for their own use that their wives and children lived in grim poverty. This phenomenon has, of course, been documented before, most notably by Rowntree, who described it as 'secondary poverty', attributed it to the 'mismanagement' of money and dealt with it in a

1

very cursory way (Rowntree, 1901). More recent work on living standards often did not mention the issue at all. I realised that the poverty of the women whom I had been interviewing would not appear in statistics about the nature and extent of poverty, because, though they were very poor, many lived in households with incomes well above the poverty line. Their hardship was concealed by the assumption that the household is an economic unit within which resources are shared equitably.

As I grew more interested in the sharing of resources within households I realised that I had stumbled on a topic which had been extraordinarily neglected by previous researchers. Those who mentioned it often did so only in order to remark on how little was known about it, and this applied equally in the fields of social policy, sociology, and economics:

We have no data about the flows of income between people within households (Central Statistical Office, 1979, p. 133).

We do not know except in the sketchiest fashion how income is distributed between people within families (Young, 1977, p. 224).

This study . . . has been unable to draw upon any specific knowledge of the nature and extent of sharing of economic resources within the household. This area of research deserves some priority (Fiegehen, Lansley and Smith, 1977, p. 118).

This was the context within which I began my investigation. Not only was this a neglected topic but it was also an extremely important one, occupying a crucial intersection between the economic and the social, between the economy outside the household and that within it. It seemed that knowing more about the control and allocation of money within the family would help in providing answers to a number of key questions. For example:

1. What are the processes which take place within households between the earning and the spending of income?

2. To what extent are the different economic situations of husbands and wives reflected in differences between 'his' marriage and 'her' marriage?

3. What are the implications of different forms of intervention by the state into the lives of married couples?

In this introductory chapter we consider each of those three questions in turn.

Between earning and spending

When a single person lives alone he or she is likely to be both the main earner and the main spender for that household. If an economist were to analyse the consumer behaviour of such an individual there would be a substantial body of economic theory on which to draw. When two or more adults live in the same household economists have traditionally treated that household as though it were an individual and have assumed that the same economic theories apply. Thus a recent text on the principles of microconomics stated:

> The basic social unit is the 'household'. This may contain one person or many, but two things will *always* be assured:
> (a) the composition of the households is *fixed* exogenously,
> (b) each household acts as an individual agent with coherent objectives. We do not question how consumption is allocated within the household (Cowell, 1986, p. 62 [italics in original]).

But can we assume that individuals and households behave in similar ways? Where one individual is the main earner and another the main spender what social and economic processes shape the allocation of money within that household?

Certainly households are key economic units, described by a leading economist as 'one of the principal groups of actors on the economic stage'; he continued,

> A typical household sells, or attempts to sell, its labour services to employers and receives as proceeds of the sale, labour income. Moreover, the household may own financial assets (such as savings certificates, shares, *etc.*) and non-financial assets (such as property) from which it also derives income. The household's income may also include payments from the government in the form of social security payments, old age pensions *etc.* With this income the household purchases goods and services, pays taxes, and, perhaps, saves (Jones, 1985, p. 29).

In reality, of course, income is earned by individuals, not households, and goods and services are purchased not by households but by individuals. However, 'by a heroic simplification the separate identities of men and women are merged into the concept of the household. The inner conflicts and compromises of the household are not explored' (Galbraith, quoted by Land, 1983, p. 49).

By treating it as though it were an individual the household has become a sort of black box, within which the transfer of resources between earners and spenders has been rendered invisible. One attempt at opening up the black box has been made by the school of thought known as the 'new home economics'. Unfortunately much of this work has used a model of the household which is both simplistic and out-dated. For example, a leading exponent of the new home economics discusses intra-household financial arrangements in terms of 'altruistic benefactors', who share their money with non-earning members of the household, and 'selfish benefactors', who consume more financial resources than they contribute (Becker, 1981). As we shall see in Chapter 7, being a breadwinner or a dependant is more complicated than this terminology would suggest.

Studies of patterns of spending have largely ignored the control and allocation of money within the household. It is usually assumed that changes in spending reflect changes in income levels, in household composition or in the 'tastes' of particular groups of consumers. The neglect of the intra-household economy is surprising, given the immense value to large corporations of any information which would help them to understand the processes which precede spending decisions. If it could be shown that financial arrangements within the household affect how much is spent, by whom and on what items, this would be of great commercial significance. This book does not aspire to make a contribution in the field of market research. However, one of its aims is to open up the black box of the household in a way which will increase our understanding of the complicated social and economic processes which occur between earning and spending.

'Her' marriage and 'his' marriage

Sociologists have traditionally been more sensitive to the analytic distinction between the household, the family and the individual. In recent years there has been a growing interest in the household as a focus for research. For example, Ray Pahl has argued that

> emphasis on the household rather than the individual as the basic
> economic unit is a more fruitful way to approach the work of production,
> reproduction and consumption (Pahl, R., 1984, p. 20).

However, this concern with the household has not prevented sociologists from examining what goes on within households and
documenting the part which gender, generation and the life course
play in structuring intra-household relationships.

It was a sociologist who first pointed to the distinction between
'his' marriage and 'her' marriage:

> There is by now a very considerable body of well-authenticated research
> to show that there really are two marriages in every marital union, and
> that they do not always coincide (Bernard, 1970, p. 20).

So it is important to recognise the tension between the couple and
the individual, and between the two individuals who make up the
couple. When two people marry they create a new social and
economic unit – a marriage – and yet they also remain two separate
individuals, as any spouse who has forgotten a wedding anniversary
can testify.

Relatively few researchers have interviewed husband and wife
separately, but those who have done so have found substantial
discrepancies between their answers (see, for example, Safilios
Rothschild, 1969; Edgell, 1980; Blumstein and Schwartz, 1983).
More often, however, researchers have investigated marriage
through the eyes of one partner, usually the wife, and have neglected
to explore the differences between being a married man and being a
married woman. It may be no accident that this omission is
paralleled by neglect, in the academic literature, of the economic
aspects of married life: the very different ways in which men and
women experience marriage are rooted in their different economic
circumstances.

There are conflicts, too, between different models of marriage. In
Europe and North America the traditional form of marriage has
grown out of a patriarchal order characterised by the rule of the
husband/father over both wife and children. The ideology of
patriarchy constructs marriage as an essentially unequal, and essentially economic relationship, expressed in the man's claim to be the
chief earner and the head of the household, while the woman has

responsibility for domestic work and child care. This pattern of marriage is sustained by the state by, for example, paying men at higher rates than women, giving married men higher tax allowances than married women, barring women, formally or informally, from the better paid jobs, offering little help with the work of child care and generally presenting femininity in terms of financial dependence and unpaid domestic work.

Patriarchal ideologies do not, of course, reign unchallenged. There have been many claims that marriage is becoming more egalitarian, more symmetrical (Young and Willmott, 1973). There is increasing evidence that assumptions about the financial dependence of married women are likely to be both inaccurate and damaging. They are inaccurate in that at any one time less than one fifth of adult women are now wholly dependent financially on a male breadwinner; they are damaging in that the ideology of women's financial dependence legitimates low pay and discriminatory tax and benefit systems (Glendinning and Millar, 1987).

A second aim of this book is to explore the changing nature of marriage, as experienced both in 'her' marriage and in 'his' marriage, and as expressed in ideologies about married life. As we shall see in chapters 2 and 3, much of the legal framework which maintained the power of men within marriage has been dismantled and women's right to control their own earnings and property is now respected by all but the most authoritarian husbands. The results of this study, as presented in chapters 4 to 9, reveal a complex picture of competing ideologies, both about the nature of marriage and about the roles of men and women within it. Ideological debates about the nature of marriage become public issues in struggles over the shape of social and economic policy, as we shall see in chapter 8.

Marriage and the state

The state is involved in regulating and controlling marriage in a variety of different ways. For the purposes of this book a crucial aspect of state policy concerns the assumptions which are made about whether two individuals who live together as a couple pool their financial resources. If the two individuals are of the same sex, or of different generations, it is usually assumed that they will not share their money. However, if they are a married couple the situation is different.

Income maintenance schemes typically assume that if a man and a woman live together they will pool their money and that he will support her financially. Thus in Britain a woman cannot continue to claim income support in her own right if a man who is earning comes to live with her; if he, too, is in receipt of income support then one of them must become the 'claimant' on behalf of the couple and any dependent children. Until 1988 the British taxation system treated husband and wife as a unit: a note on the first page of the 1987 Tax Return read, 'If you are a married man and your wife is living with you, you must show all her income and chargeable gains and assets acquired'. Though a wife could opt for separate assessment of earnings, any income she received from savings was deemed to be part of the husband's income. This meant that husbands could keep their financial position secret from their partners in a way that wives could not. The idea of the 'family wage' also assumes the sharing of resources. Fought for by the Labour movement and opposed by many feminists, this idea suggests that a man should be able to earn enough to support himself, his wife and children at a decent level. The family wage has been attacked both because if it were to be achieved it would exacerbate the dependence of married women, and also because those who fought for it never seemed to question the extent to which the wage would in reality be shared with other members of the family (Barrett and McIntosh, 1980; Land, 1980).

In other spheres individuals living as couples are not necessarily expected to be pooling their resources. In 1988 Britain moved to a system of independent taxation for husband and wife: the implications of this will be discussed in chapter 8. The payment of child benefit to all mothers reflects a recognition that some fathers do not contribute to the costs of rearing their children. Wages and salaries are paid to individuals, not to couples or households. This is in contrast to the situation observed in parts of nineteenth-century France where some wives, as financial managers of peasant households, negotiated wage rates on behalf of their husbands and received pay packets directly from their employers (Le Play, 1855). Under British common law there is no concept of 'community property' within marriages, as there is in many other parts of the world. Divorce reveals the reality which lies behind the assumption that couples pool their resources. A growing body of research has shown that when marriages end women and children typically receive a meagre share of the husband's resources, if they receive anything at all (Eekelaar and Maclean, 1986; Dobash and Wasoff, 1986; Weitzman, 1985). Summarising research on the financial impact of marital breakdown Millar concluded:

> While the family income may be 'theirs' during marriage (and thus the distribution of income within the family can be ignored), if the marriage breaks down it becomes clear that it was really 'his' all along (Millar, 1987, p. 105).

However, this study is not about divorce but about intact marriages. There has been little legislation specifically concerned with the allocation of money within marriage; this is usually explained by reference to the private nature of marriage and the inappropriateness of outside interference. However, this has not prevented the passing of legislation which has reflected assumptions about how married couples allocate their money, and which is likely to reinforce particular patterns of allocation.

The process of economic development raises the issue of the intervention of the state into marriage in a particularly significant way. Development may take the form of subsistence agriculture giving way to the growing of cash crops, or of peasant farmers moving to urban areas to find employment in factories or service industries. All these transitions tend to involve an increase in the importance of money as a way of providing for needs. Yet money income typically accrues to individuals, rather than to households or couples. So when development occurs, whether it be funded by private investment or by aid agencies, what are the implications for the financial arrangements of those involved?

Aid agencies have all too often ignored this issue. They have worked on the assumption that the household can be treated as a unit within which resources are shared equitably: it does not matter who earns or spends the money, nor does it matter if one household member gains and another loses from the process of development. The damage done by this assumption has been compounded by the fact that aid agencies have also tended to approach developing countries with stereotypes drawn from a masculine view of European and North American bourgeois society. This has meant that women have been offered classes in child care, nutrition and hygiene, while men have been given material aid, such as agricultural machinery, seeds and fertilisers. The effect has been to decrease the resources controlled by women and to increase those controlled by men. Recent years have seen the publication of a substantial body of research on the implications of this process (Dwyer and Bruce, 1988; Blumberg, 1988; Carloni, 1987; Leghorn and Parker, 1981; Rogers, 1980; Rogers, 1984).

The process of economic development raises a number of questions which are also central to this book. Are resources pooled within households, and if they are not, what distinguishes pooling from non-pooling households? If money is not pooled, or is only partly pooled, does it matter whether that money is earned by a man or a woman? Given the same level of income, do women or men contribute a greater proportion to the common purse? Which earners are likely to keep the largest proportion of their income back for personal use? Do men and women have different priorities for spending? And does an individual who contributes more money to the household also have more power when it comes to making household decisions? This book is focussed mainly on Britain. However, its topic raises questions which are relevant in every country throughout the world.

Definitions

Finally, this seems the appropriate point at which to define some key terms. The 'household' has been defined as 'either one person living alone, or a group of people (who may or may not be related) living at the same address with common housekeeping' (Central Statistical Office, 1983, p. 192). Thus the household is primarily an economic unit, characterised by common residence and at least some sharing of resources. Defining the term 'family' is more problematic. In one sense it is a biological unit, in which kinship plays a central part. However, the family has assumed so many different forms in the course of history that it has to be seen primarily as a social rather than a biological construction (Mitterauer and Sieder, 1982; Morgan, 1985). Precise definitions tend to say little about all the different meanings of the word 'family', while saying a lot about the cultural norms and ideological stance of the person making the definition. The 'families' with which this study was concerned consisted of two parents, who were married in all but one case, all of whom had at least one dependent child living with them in the same household. In the pages which follow the words 'household' and 'family' will often be used interchangeably. However, it is important to remember that both households and families can take many different forms. The extent to which money is shared within other sorts of social groups offers a rich field for further research.

2
The legal framework

The traditional vow made by the bridegroom in the Church of England wedding ceremony was a direct contradiction of the legal changes which marriage entailed, especially for the wife. The husband who stood in church and promised 'with all my wordly goods I thee endow' was in truth taking possession of his wife's goods and all her future earnings, because until the late nineteenth century marriage marked the point at which a woman's property passed into the hands of her husband. It is through following the changing legal status of the married woman that we can trace the legal and ideological construction of property relations within marriage. In his classic history of English law, Holdsworth commented:

> The status of the married woman is one of the most difficult of all the problems of private law; and to it legal systems have given, and still give, the most diverse answers. No legal system which deals merely with human rules of contract desires to pry too closely into the relationship of husband and wife. Dealings between husband and wife are for the most part privileged (Holdsworth, 1923, p. 520).

The 'privileged' nature of the relationship has meant that legal systems have said little on the specific topic of the allocation of money within marriage: in general the law is more concerned with financial arrangements at the start of marriage or at its ending. However, it is important to outline the assumptions which the law has made about the legal status of married women since this has provided the framework, both legal and normative, within which decisions about marital property have been made.

11

There is a crucial distinction between two different systems of law: common law and equity. While the common law was pre-eminent throughout the Middle Ages, equity developed from the sixteenth century onwards, in part as a response to changing social and economic conditions. The two systems of law were based on very different assumptions about the nature of marriage. In her detailed discussion of the two systems of law and of their provisions in regard to matrimonial property, Holcombe concluded that both the common law and equity proceeded upon the assumption that married women needed protection. The common law regarded a woman's husband as her guardian, under whose 'wing, protection and cover' she lived, moved and had no legal being. But equity, generally considered to be 'the guardian of the weak and unprotected, such as married women, infants and lunatics', tended to view a woman's husband as 'the enemy' and against his exorbitant rights the Court of Chancery waged constant war (Holcombe, 1983, p. 37).

The common law

Until the late nineteenth century the position was that, under the common law, marriage meant that husband and wife became one person, so that the legal existence of the woman was incorporated into that of her husband. This implied that any property which a woman possessed or was entitled to at the time of her marriage, and any property which she became entitled to after it, became her husband's to control. Any will made by a single woman was revoked by marriage, because her husband then took over her property, and any will that she might subsequently make had to have his consent. Husband and wife could not make gifts to each other since, by the act of marrying, a woman had in effect made a gift of her property to her husband, while the fact that a married woman could not hold property prevented her husband from making over anything into her possession. Legally, a married woman was a *'feme covert'*, whose legal identity was covered by that of her husband.

There has been some speculation about the origin of the common law notion that marriage suspended the legal identity of the married woman and deprived her of her right to hold property. Some have argued that the common law position embodied the sacramental view of marriage held by the medieval church, according to which marriage made two persons one flesh and made wives submit to the authority of their husbands. On the other hand, other historians have argued that the common law reflected the economic and social realities of the Middle Ages, the time when the law was developed. When most people derived their livelihood from the land, which was worked by all the members of the household, or from producing goods at home for domestic use, a husband's control of his wife's property could be seen as a way of protecting the interests of the household as a whole.

The common law recognised various different categories of property and applied different rules to each. The two most important categories were 'real property' which consisted of property in the form of freehold and copyhold land, and 'personal property', also known as chattels personal, corporeal chattels and choses in possession, which consisted of tangible objects other than land. The common law afforded married women considerable protection with respect to real property, but little or no protection to personal property. As far as real property was concerned, the common law made it clear that the husband was the guardian of the property and not its legal owner. If the land was to be disposed of during the marriage the wife had to be examined separately in court in order to determine whether she agreed freely to the disposition of her land. If a wife survived her husband her real property reverted to her control, while she also had the right to a life interest in her husband's lands. If a wife died before her husband the land passed not to him, but to her heirs as specified by statute, though by the 'curtesy of England' he had a right to a life interest in her land.

The position with regard to the wife's personal property was very different. Whether the property took the form of earnings or savings, clothes or furniture, a factory or a shop, the husband could dispose of or use the property in any way he chose. As legal owner of the property he could, without his wife's consent, bequeath it by will. A wife, however, could only make a will with her husband's consent and if she died without making a will her personal property continued to be her husband's absolutely, to the exclusion of her children or other relatives. Under common law, until the late nineteenth century, the husband was the legal representative of his wife. It was seen as natural and just that the law should give a husband ownership of and control over his wife's property, in order to help him to fulfil his obligation to support his wife and children.

However, if a husband failed in this obligation, his wife was unable to charge him with non-support since legally they were one person and could not sue each other. If a wife took paid work in order to support herself and her children, her earnings were legally the property of her husband and he could dispose of the money as he pleased.

The history of the common law in relation to matrimonial property is extremely complicated and it is only possible to provide a brief summary here. (For more extensive discussion, see Craik, 1984; Holcombe, 1983; Holdsworth, 1923–1966; O'Donovan, 1985.) Holdsworth saw the issue in patriarchal terms, that is in terms of balancing the rights of the wife and children to be protected and supported against the right of the husband to exercise his power as head of the family:

> It is not right that the family property should be squandered: at the same time it is advisable to give the husband a free hand in its management – he is the head of the family. The problem is to draw the line in such a way as to preserve something for the wife and family without unduly fettering the powers of the husband (Holdsworth, 1923, p. 521).

Taking a very broad view of the many various answers which have been given to this problem, the lawyers of Western Europe recognised two main systems. On the one hand there were those countries which recognised a system of community of ownership between husband and wife; these included parts of what is now Spain and Germany and south-west France. On the other hand there were parts of Europe where community of ownership was not assumed but where the husband was seen as the legal owner of his wife's property. These areas included most of England, parts of what is now Italy, and Normandy and eastern France. In Britain it was only in Kent, through the system of gavelkind, that husband and wife enjoyed a type of community of property (Goody, 1976; Robinson, 1788). It is interesting to speculate briefly on the implications of each of these two systems for relationships within marriage. To what extent did the long history of community of property in certain parts of Europe contribute to giving women greater power within marriage? Did community of property give married women a greater sense of self esteem and autonomy, in comparison with the 'dwindling into a wife' experienced by women who had to relinquish their property on marriage?

In England the common law developed slowly. Holdsworth suggested that in the twelfth century the law had still not made up its mind as to the position of the married woman and could have moved towards a system of community of property. He cited examples of wives who carried on trade in their own names, who made wills, and who inherited on the death of their husbands (Holdsworth, 1923, p. 523). However, from the thirteenth century onwards the law moved away from any theory of community of matrimonial property. The husband became legally the guardian and controller of his wife's real property and the absolute owner of her personal property. Since a married woman had no personal property it was impossible for her to make legal contracts. In the reign of Henry VII her legal position was set out by Fineux:

> If a married woman makes a contract, or buys anything in the market, the contract is void ... But if my wife can buy a thing to my use, and I can ratify that; and so, if I command my wife to buy necessaries, and she buys them, I shall be bound by reason of my general authority given to her. And if my wife buys things for my household, such as bread, *etc.*, and I know nothing of it, even though they be consumed in my household, I shall not on that account be charged (Fineux, C.J. Quoted in Holdsworth, 1923).

This principle was modified in an important respect in 1707 when it was decided in the case of *James* v. *Warren* that if a man wrongfully deserted his wife, and left her destitute, she was his 'agent of necessity' and could pledge his credit for necessaries (Holdsworth, 1923). The wife's right to pledge her husband's credit in order to buy necessities for herself and her children remained in force till 1970. In practice this right provided little protection to women, since few shopkeepers relished the idea of suing a reluctant husband for the value of goods supplied to his wife, however needy she might be.

The legal position of married women seems to have meant that, at least in theory, women were not expected to be in control of money. Evidence for this assertion comes from a study of English books for women published in the period 1475 to 1640 (Hull, 1982). These books ranged from prayer books to romances; about half took the form of practical guides on such topics as how to educate girls, how to treat servants, how to write letters, how to cook and sew and garden. Of the 85 practical guides, 84 were written by men and 22 took the form of cookery books. None of the 85 dealt directly with keeping accounts or with the management of money. The only book which dealt with financial matters was *The Lawes Resolutions of Womens Rights: or, the Lawes Provision for Woemen* (1632). This was the first legal textbook devoted exclusively to the legal position of women. The merging of her legal identity into that of her husband is shown in the case of rape:

> If a Femme covert be ravished, shee cannot have an Appeale without her husband, as appears 8.Hen.4. fol.21. But if a Feme covert be ravished and consent to the ravisher, the husband alone may have an Appeale, and this by the Statute of 6.Rich.2.cap.6 (ET, 1632, p. 390).

The husband's control over his wife's personal property is discussed under the heading 'That which the Wife hath is her Husband's':

> For thus it is, if before Marriage the woman were possessed of Horses, Meate, Sheepe, Coyne, Wool, Money or Plate and Jewels, all manner of moveable substance is presently by conjunction the husbands, to sell, keepe or bequeath if he die: And though he bequeath them not, yet they are the Husband's Executors and not the wives which brought them to her Husband (ET, 1632, p. 130).

Thus under the common law, from the Middle Ages to the late nineteenth century, a wife had no right to own personal property, and any land which she might bring to a marriage was legally under the control of her husband.

Equity

Any discussion of the legal position of the married woman must take account, however, of the alternative body of law developed under the system of equity. Two explanations for this development were put forward by Holcombe (1983). First, if the common law rules, based on the fused identity of husband and wife, reflected the sacramental view of marriage held by the medieval church, then equity followed from the breakdown of the power of the church at the reformation and the growth of Protestant sects which saw marriage as a civil contract. Secondly, Holcombe suggested that the development of the equity system was the consequence of changing economic and social conditions. The growth of new social classes, whose wealth derived not from land but from commerce and industry, meant that the common law was unable to protect the property of daughters from the predations of husbands. The common law had provided some protection for property in the form of land, but it provided no protection for all other forms of property. Wealthy families became increasingly concerned to ensure that family property which passed to a daughter should either pass to her children or return to another member of her family of origin.

In order to meet the needs of these wealthy families, lawyers developed the trust system of property, known as equity. Originally, trusts were private arrangements unrecognised by the common law and unenforceable in the common law courts. One example of this early form of trust comes from the will of Alice Lord, made on 12 April 1610, in the section concerned with the disposition of her property:

> I dare not give it to my sonne in law William Shipton for that I have allwaies found him an evil husband both to his wief and for his estate and therefore onlie I give him 10s. and all the rest of my goods I bequeath to my loveinge friends Mr John Dod, Mr Robert Cleaver, Mr Rowland Bull, William Goodall and Ralph Carter, in trust for my daughter Ann Shipton (Vann, 1979, p. 357).

The increasing size of the sums involved in wills must have given rise to doubt as to whether informal arrangements with friends could provide adequate protection for the property of wives. So from the sixteenth century onwards the law of equity in relation to property in trust was developed: such property was protected by the Court of Chancery against a woman's husband and all other persons according to the wishes of the donor. Any type of property, in common law terms both real property and personal property, could be covered by equity.

The rights which a married woman had over property held in trust for her depended on the provisions of the trust. In some cases a woman had unrestricted rights over her property, but in other instances restrictions were placed on her forbidding her to sell or give away the property, or withdrawing her right to it if she committed adultery or left her husband without good cause. Since trusts were typically set up by fathers for their daughters, with trustees drawn from a woman's male relatives, there is a sense in which equity law, too, defined women as controlled by and dependent on men. This view of equity law was justified on the grounds that women could not be trusted to manage their own finances sensibly. It was expressed by the Attorney-General, speaking in a debate on married women's rights to property which took place in the House of Lords on 10 June 1868:

> The right hon. gentleman says that women in the upper classes are protected by a settlement made before marriage, and that this is the best proof of the errors and wickednesses of the common law. But marriage settlements are framed not only to protect the wife, but to take care that on her part she does not make away with the property and prevent the children of the marriage being benefited by it. A marriage settlement is never made for the benefit and protection of the wife alone (Hear, hear) (*The Times*, 11 June 1868, p. 6).

Taken together, the two systems of law demonstrate very neatly the interlocking inequalities of gender and class. In common law the property of married women was controlled by their husbands, while in equity it was protected against husbands by the continuing power of fathers, uncles and brothers. In both forms of law married women were unable to control their own property, unless permission to do so had been given by a man. Thus class inequalities modified the nature of the subordination experienced by all married women. The property of poor women, which mainly took the form of earnings and of meagre amounts of clothing and household goods, was covered by the common law, while the greater protection offered by equity was only available to women in the propertied classes.

Women from wealthy families might retain some rights over their property through the provisions of equity. However, these represented a small minority, and even in the mid-nineteenth century, when equity was well developed as a body of law, marriage settlements applied to only one tenth of marriages (*Hansard*, 1856, p. 410). The reason for this was that proceedings in the courts of equity were very expensive, with the cost of drawing up a marriage settlement amounting to over £100, this being only one of the expenses involved. As a result, it was impractical to tie up small sums of money in trust settlements. Most importantly, for all women their earnings from employment were legally the property of their husbands.

Nineteenth-century reforms

Dissatisfaction with the shortcomings of both common law and equity, and with the discrepancies between them, were among the main causes of the campaign to reform the law relating to the property of married women. This movement began in the 1850s and achieved its most substantial success with the passing of the Married Women's Property Act in 1882. In his study of the nineteenth century movement for legal reform, Dicey argued that the reform of married women's property law was prompted by the increase in the number of wage earning wives (Dicey, 1920). The lack of statistics means that it is difficult to document the growth in the numbers of wives in employment over the first half of the century, but by 1851 there were 838,856 married women in paid jobs, representing nearly a quarter of all employed women.

An early task of the campaigners for reform was to publicise the consequences of the legal handicaps which affected married women. In her account of the movement for reform, Holcombe cites a number of individual examples which achieved public attention in the 1850s:

A lady was deserted by her husband, who went off with another woman to Australia to seek his fortune in the gold fields. She opened a school in order to support herself, but her husband, having failed in his venture, returned to England and seized all her property.

A woman was cruelly treated by her husband, who was at last convicted by a court of assault on her. Meanwhile her father died, leaving her considerable property. But the husband was the legal owner, and since he was a convicted felon the property was forfeited to the crown.

A woman whose husband had failed in business set up a fashionable millinery establishment with a few friends. So successful was the venture that she made a considerable fortune and retired from business to live on her savings. Meanwhile her husband did not work, and she supported him. When he died, he left a will bequeathing her property to his illegitimate children so that she was left penniless and had to become a milliner again (Holcombe, 1983, p. 66).

Despite the injustice inherent in cases such as these, the opposition to reform persisted over the following 25 years. Between 1857 and 1882 no less than 20 separate bills directed at reforming the law relating to the property of married women were introduced in the

House of Commons. Only five succeeded in receiving the royal assent. Of these five, two were essentially concerned with protecting the interests of the male business community by removing the husband's liability for his wife's pre-nuptial debts. Commenting on the swift and easy passage of these two bills, Holcombe wrote:

> Women might well ponder the ease and speed with which a bill to remedy the grievances of the male business community was passed, compared to the unsuccessful attempts to remedy their own grievances (Holcombe, 1983, p. 191).

Opponents of reform argued that the subordination of women within marriage was both traditional and natural; they suggested that a change in the law would lead to revolutionary changes in family life and in the relations between men and women. A series of quotations from *Times* leaders of the late 1860s illustrates some of these points:

> The proposed legislation would completely recast the relations of men and women in the married state ... As in the eyes of the Church the two become one flesh, so in the eyes of the law they become one person. The husband took and answered for all; the wife gave up everything, but obtained in return a guarantee against wanting anything. That, in general terms, was the theory of marriage in its financial aspect ... The pending bill was intended to protect the earnings of married women in the humbler classes of life from the hands of selfish, reckless and extravagant husbands. From this point of view, therefore, there is a consistency about the proposal. If a wife takes a share in man's work, she may ask a share in man's privilege. The old theory of the man being the breadwinner and the woman the housewife disappears when she brings home an income of 4L or 5L a week, and there are, we are told, 800,000 women who are actually in receipt of wages more or less in amount ... But could it be thought sound policy to upset the whole relations of marriage for the sake of a particular class of wives (*The Times*, 12 June 1868, p. 9).

It is interesting to note that this leader writer, like many a commentator in the late twentieth century, harks back to an 'old theory' according to which the man was the breadwinner and the woman the housewife. It seems that the idea of the earning wife as a modern aberration has a long history, perhaps because it is a convenient device for making the earnings of wives appear both marginal and unreliable.

The men who wrote the *Times* leaders saw clearly the links

between financial arrangements within marriage and the nature of the relationship between husband and wife, and they were stalwart defenders of the *status quo*:

> We believe, with Lord Penzance, that the essential idea of the married state is one of subordination; and if so, it must be a matter of grave doubt whether the law regulating it ought to be based on the idea of equality. The theories now afloat respecting the equality of the sexes and the independence of women have not yet received the sanction, even if they have received the consideration of the English people. Our present law is rough, as the inheritance of rough times, and the great task of legislation is to adapt it to more delicate circumstances. But rude justice is often substantially just; and for our part, we are disposed to think that the sentiments of our forefathers on the present question afford an eminent instance of this rule (*The Times*, 31 July 1869, p. 9).

The opponents of reform waged a skilful and emotive rearguard action, using all the delaying tactics which Parliamentary procedures afforded them.

Two acts transformed the legal position of married women. The first was the Married Women's Property Act of 1870, which made it possible for married women without marriage settlements to hold property in their own right. However, the property which they could hold was limited. First and most important, married women were to have the right to hold the wages and earnings from any employment, occupation or trade. Secondly, they could hold money invested in specific ways, which included government stocks and funds, building and loan societies and life assurance. Thirdly, married women could hold money coming to them by inheritance, but there were qualifications to this provision, the most important being that any inheritance over £200 still legally belonged to the husband. The inadequacies of the Married Women's Property Act of 1870 meant that married women still did not have the same rights to property as men and single women, and as such the Act was a bitter disappointment to those who had fought so hard for reform. It was not until 1882 that the long struggle waged by feminists, and their supporters in Parliament, was finally rewarded by the passing of the Married Women's Property Act.

The effect of the Married Women's Property Act of 1882 was to give married women the same rights over property as men and unmarried women. It covered every sort of property, of whatever kind and from whatever source, which a woman possessed at the time of marriage or to which she became entitled after marriage. Married women were also specifically empowered to carry on trades and businesses separately from their husbands, using their separate property. The Act did not interfere with existing settlements under equity, but every married woman without a settlement was to hold all her property as her separate property, as though she were a *feme sole*. The Act was thus in harmony with contemporary concern that the common law and equity should be fused and that in the event of a conflict between them equity should prevail.

The Married Women's Property Acts can be seen as the greatest transfer of resources from married men to married women which has ever taken place. The calculation was set out by Lord Shaftesbury during a debate in 1870. He estimated that if approximately 800,000 wives were employed at wages of an average £20 per year, then £16,000,000 was the sum currently earned by women but belonging to men. To this he added £16,000,000 worth of property other than earnings which wives had brought to their husbands through marriage. The result is to make 1882 as important a date in the history of the reallocation of property as the dissolution of the monasteries (*Hansard*, 1870, p. 397).

Twentieth century law

Though the 1882 Act can be seen as a great victory for feminists, and for women, it did not, of course, achieve anything like equality. Most importantly, perhaps, it did little to alter the financial dependence of wives on their husbands.

The only existing legislation which deals directly with the allocation of money within marriage is the Married Women's Property Act 1964. This provides that any savings from a housekeeping allowance given by a husband to a wife belong equally to them both. The situation before the Act came into force was that such savings belonged to the husband, since the wife was deemed to be acting as his agent. Since 1964 the legal status of money transferred between husband and wife has depended on the purpose for which the transfer is made and the person initiating the transfer. If there is evidence that the transfer is a gift then it becomes the property of the person to whom it is given. If a wife gives money to her husband for household purposes it appears that the money becomes his and that he can keep any savings from it, unless there is evidence of a contrary agreement (Law Commission, 1985, p. 3). However, under the 1964 Act, money given by a husband to a wife for household purposes does not become hers but remains jointly theirs: thus the present law relating to the transfer of money between spouses discriminates against women.

It has been suggested that the 1964 Act should be replaced by a provision to the effect that where money is made available, directly or indirectly, by the spouse for the joint purposes of the spouses, this money and any property acquired with it, should in the absence of any agreement to the contrary be owned equally by both spouses (Law Commission, 1985, p. 26). It has been argued that this would abolish any lingering suggestion that a wife acts merely as her husband's agent when she spends housekeeping money. The proposal has many important implications. One major effect would be that many more household goods, including the matrimonial home, would automatically be jointly owned. Where a couple had a joint account, the money placed in the account and any property bought with it, whether for joint purposes or not, would be jointly owned, in the absence of agreement to the contrary. However, this proposal stops short of advocating the more general co-ownership implied in community property systems.

In a community property system the earnings of both partners, together with all other property acquired during the marriage, except inheritances and gifts, become 'community property'. Each spouse owns one half of this community property. The system thus implies that both spouses have contributed equally to the economic assets of their marriage, whether by homemaking or by earning a salary, and that each is entitled to an equal share of the total assets. If a marriage ends in divorce the full-time housewife is much better off under a community property system than under the common law, where there is an underlying assumption that the husband, as earner, is also the owner of all the property acquired during the marriage.

Both France and West Germany offer their citizens a choice in the way they hold their matrimonial property: unless the couple choose to make a marriage contract a community property system will exist. This means that the agreement of both partners is needed for all major financial transactions. The wife can claim against community funds for reasonable household expenses and has the power to veto financial decisions made by her husband. Either spouse may be held responsible to the community for mismanagement of the property. Many countries with a tradition based on British common law are now moving towards a greater degree of community of property in marriage; the implications of this have been explored more fully by O'Donovan (1985) and Weitzman (1985). Meanwhile in Britain the right of a wife to financial support extends only to her keep and does not entitle her to any particular share of her husband's income.

The history of the husband's obligation to maintain his wife was summarised by Finer and McGregor in their evidence to the Finer Committee (Department of Health and Social Security, 1977, p. 85). Until the nineteenth century the common law recognised the husband's obligation to support his wife, but did not give her any right to enforce the obligation if he did not maintain her or their children. When it was first granted the wife's right to maintenance could only be enforced when the couple were living separately. The Matrimonial Causes Act 1857 provided that, when a marriage was dissolved, the divorce court could order the husband to pay a gross sum, or annual payments to the wife. The Matrimonial Causes Act 1878 extended the right to maintenance to poorer women by making it possible for a wife to take her case to a magistrates' court. However, it was not till 1925 that a court could order a husband to pay maintenance while the couple were still living in the same house. The Summary Jurisdiction (Separation and Maintenance) Act gave a wife the right to obtain an order on the ground of wilful neglect to maintain, even though she was not living apart from her husband, although the order lapsed if she was still living with him three months after it was made.

The right of the husband to be supported by his wife was recognised in the Act of 1882 but husbands were not given the same access to the magistrates' courts until very much later. The Matrimonial Proceedings (Magistrates Courts) Act of 1960 gave to a husband the right to obtain an order for his wife to maintain him, but maintenance was only granted if a husband could prove that his earning power had been reduced through age or illness. The situation remains one in which the husband's duty to maintain his wife is a normal incidence of marriage, whilst her obligation to maintain him results from abnormal and pathological situations (Kahn-Freund, 1971, p. 494).

Under the Domestic Proceedings and Magistrates' Courts Act of 1978 (s.i) the spouses have a mutual duty of financial support. However, so long as a couple live together, the court cannot force one partner to support another for more than a short period. A magistrates' court order, if made while the partners are cohabiting, ceases if they continue to live together for more than three months, and if made while they are apart, ceases immediately on resumption of cohabitation (Eekelaar, 1978, p. 250). The courts have refused to define what a reasonable housekeeping allowance from husband to wife might be. Despite the emphasis in pay negotiations on the idea of the 'family wage', in English law there is no legal obligation on the primary wage earner to share his or her earnings with the other spouse.

It is significant that the legal changes which took place in England in the late nineteenth and early twentieth centuries were not influenced by the rather different property régimes to be found in the rest of Europe. The common law of Scotland, from medieval times to the nineteenth century, provided for a form of community property between spouses, while in many other European countries the law recognised some sort of partnership or community of assets. In England, on the other hand, married women's property rights were enlarged by reference to a principle of equality, which had the effect of individualising those rights (Finer and McGregor, 1975, p. 111). It might be argued that since under traditional English law husband and wife became one person, this constituted a form of community property. However, community property implies two-way rights, so that a woman has rights in her husband's property as well as he in hers. On the other hand, under English law the husband simply took possession of his wife's property, at least so long as the marriage lasted. It might be thought that a community property system would be to the advantage of wives on divorce. However, research carried out in the United States has shown that the combination of a no-fault divorce law with a community property system has led to a situation in which women of all ages and at all socio-economic levels experience a precipitous decline in their standard of living within one year of divorce, while their former husbands' standard of living improves (Weitzman, 1985, p. 400).

The ideology expressed in modern common law, as it relates to matrimonial property in England and Wales, is one which sees marriage as the joining together of two individuals, rather than as

the creation of a new unit, the couple. In this respect the law relating
to matrimonial property differs markedly from the law relating to
social security in which husband and wife are typically assumed to
be a unit within which property is pooled.

In this chapter we have been concerned with the law as it relates to
the property of husbands and wives within marriage. There are, of
course, complicated and extensive areas of the law dealing with the
amalgamation of property at the start of a marriage and with the
distribution of property when a marriage ends through death or
divorce. However, these other areas of the law have to be neglected,
since the main focus of the book is on the control and allocation of
money within existing marriages. In the next chapter we turn from
the theory to the practice, from the provisions of the law to the
everyday arrangements which married men and women have made
at different historical periods about their earnings and savings, their
income and their capital.

3

The historical evidence

The historical evidence suggests that family financial arrangements have varied widely, according to such variables as place and time, social class and income level, life cycle stage and household type, and the ways in which work has been organised and income received. Though historical material is scattered, and often tangential there is a great deal of it. So, in spite of the availability of fascinating material from other parts of the world, and from other parts of the British Isles, the discussion in this chapter has been limited to historical evidence drawn from England, in the period from the thirteenth century to the early twentieth century. This is itself a very broad span. The aim in this chapter will be to establish links between the experiences of individuals within families and the social and economic structures within which the lives of those families were located.

Reconstructing historical patterns of the allocation of money between husband and wife poses considerable problems. First, there is the problem of investigating a topic which was not recognised as important by most of those who compiled the historical source material on which we must draw. This does not mean that the way in which money was allocated within families was not seen as important by those most closely affected. The evidence from oral history and from working class autobiographies shows that for many nineteenth century women the problems of poverty were exacerbated by the fact that a proportion of the income of the household was diverted to the individual needs of the male breadwinner. Evidence from this source tends to take the form of sons and daughters reminiscing about their mothers' struggles, and it is clear that the allocation of money was an important issue in many working class homes, for women and children if not for men.

Other sources of evidence tend to have been compiled by people who did not recognise that the allocation of money within the family might be a problematic issue, and who were, in any case, concerned with recording rather different aspects of life. Under this heading comes a wide variety of historical sources, from the account books of families, farms and businesses to the records of the daily management of great estates, and from court rolls to the wills and inventories left by individuals on death. Additionally, there are sources which deal with the theory rather than with the practice of the allocation of money. Into this category come books of advice to young married women, literature designed to improve the domestic skills of housewives, and philosophical and moralistic works dealing with marriage and family life. Most importantly, too, there are the legal sources, both setting out the law and commenting upon it. Though in one sense these come into the category of theoretical statements about the allocation of money within the family, they are of central importance in structuring the position of women within marriage and in shaping norms and values.

Secondly, there is the problem of looking at historical sources through modern eyes. Not only were the records compiled by people who typically did not see the allocation of money between husband and wife as significant, but also we are reading the records from a viewpoint which is shaped by our own norms and coloured by our particular ideological position. This means that many of the questions which we might ask of the historical material risk being dangerously anachronistic. Not only is the historical evidence off-target but so, too, are our questions. Thus it might seem appropriate to ask how much housekeeping money middle class Victorian men gave their wives, or whether seventeenth century women left more to sons or daughters in their wills. But, as we shall see, questions such as these make assumptions about housekeeping money and wills which are misleading, if not meaningless, in the historical context to which they are applied.

Thirdly, there is the perennial problem of the historian who seeks to reconstruct the past from the scattered and fragmentary evidence which has come down to us. We are dealing with a complicated topic, which has traditionally been one of the most secret areas of family life. What weight should we attach to different sorts of evidence? How much imagination ought we to allow ourselves in bridging the gaps in our knowledge? So much historical evidence essentially relates to individuals, and it is always hard to know to what extent individual accounts and experiences can be taken as typical of wider patterns. Encouraged by Gramsci's assertion that 'if you are not able to understand real individuals, you can't under-stand what is universal and general' (Lawner, 1973, p. 136), the rest of this chapter considers the historical evidence about patterns of allocation of money in England.

The allocation of money in England before the industrial revolution

Legally the income of both husband and wife belonged to the husband from the early Middle Ages up until 1882. In practice, however, many wives were involved in managing the financial affairs of the household to a greater or lesser extent and most were responsible for certain areas of household expenditure. What aspects of household finances were most likely to be managed by wives? In what circumstances did control shift from husband to wife, or *vice versa*? And is it historically accurate to see the allocation of money within the family in terms of management and control, or would other terms be more appropriate? The word *control* will be used to indicate overall direction of the finances of the household, incorporating the notion of ownership of the money or property under discussion; the word *management* will be used to indicate administration of household finances, an activity which includes the payment of bills for daily living expenses.

The evidence suggests that the financial control and management of great estates was almost entirely in the hands of men, whether as owners or as stewards on behalf of the owner. Where large enter-prises are concerned, financial management becomes a specialised and well-rewarded job and typically such work tends to become a male preserve. When women who were the daughters or widows of wealthy men married they often brought substantial assets to the marriage in the form of land or dower, but these assets usually came under the control and management of the husband or his agent. There were exceptions to this pattern when domestic or political crises caused a husband to entrust the management of the estate to his wife. This was particularly likely to happen in war time, when the enforced absence of a husband, for example on the Crusades, could leave the making of financial decisions and the running of the estate in the hands of his wife.

However, some wives continued to control the property which they brought to the marriage, especially in the early Middle Ages before the incorporation of the wife's legal identity into that of her husband became clearly codified. Evidence for this comes from the *Household Roll of Eleanor, Countess of Leicester*, for the year 1265. The Countess had been widowed when her first husband, the Earl of Pembroke, died in 1231. She inherited many valuable and extensive manors, with an annuity of £400 payable out of the Irish estates of the family. She seems to have kept control of all this property when she married the Earl of Leicester, and the Household Roll sets out the accounts as administered by her steward. The Earl and the Countess of Leicester each had an independent income of their own and expenditure which was accounted for separately: thus the financial management of their household in Odiham was in some respects similar to the independent management system used by some young professionals in late twentieth century England (see chapter 5). When Earl Simon and his enormous retinue visited the Earl and Countess of Leicester at Odiham just before Easter 1265, the expenses for the first day of the visit were charged to the Countess' account; all the costs for the following two weeks were charged to the Earl and presumably were listed in detail on his account (Turner, 1841; Labarge, 1980, p. 57).

Among the nobility and gentry, a man's major concern was with the efficient management of his estate. In the late sixteenth century the separate roles of husband and wife were delineated:

> the man to get, to travaile abroad, to defende: the wife, to save that which is gotten, to tarrie at home to distribute that which commeth of the husbandes labor ... and to keepe all at home neat and cleane (Smith, 1583, p. 12).

Among larger landowners, both control and management of money, as evidenced by the keeping of accounts, seems to have been largely in male hands. Thus, for example, Millicent Heritage married Peter Temple, a Warwickshire farmer, in 1541 and brought to the marriage pastureland in Burton Dassett and property in Coventry and Stepney. She also brought the account book kept by her late husband and both this book, and the accounts kept by her second husband, have survived. The accounts show that Peter Temple farmed his wife's land as his own and that he was responsible for paying household bills for such staple items as 'bred and drinke, fuell, candells, salt, otemell, venegar, fleshe and fyshe'. Millicent Heritage barely figures in the accounts, except in passing in items such as 'hose for my wyffe' and 'slippers for my wyfe' (Alcock, 1981). A rather similar pattern can be seen in the accounts kept from 1616 to 1704 by Nicholas Toke and his nephew, also Nicholas Toke, for their estate at Great Chart in Kent (Lodge, 1927).

Though typically the accounts of larger farms were kept by men in the period between the sixteenth century and the nineteenth century, there are instances of women both keeping accounts and making major financial decisions. One example of this is the *Household Account Book of Sarah Fell of Swaithmore Hall* (Penney, 1920). Sarah Fell was the daughter of Margaret and George Fell, whose family included one son and six daughters. George Fell died in 1659 and ten years later his widow married George Fox, the founder of the Quakers. The only son died in 1670 and in 1673 Sarah began keeping the accounts of their Lake District farm. Again the accounts convey a vivid picture of the life of the household. For example, in the first week of May 1675 the household sold '29 hoggs, a pair of oxen and two old cows, wheat, cheese, cloth, a cabbage and a "seacocke".' Items which were purchased included a horse, wood, bread, meat, fish, some scissors, gloves and a little comb; in addition Sarah recorded that she paid money for spinning yarn and for the funeral of Brother John, lent money to one man, gave to a poor man, and finally paid her sister's maid's wages of £13.0.0 per year.

Though it was unusual for women to keep accounts on larger farms, this household was itself unusual in various other ways. The only man in the house was a second husband, who had attached himself to an establishment which was already running efficiently and who, as his journal shows, was away most of the time preaching (Fox, 1765). According to the common law all the money of the household was his; but in practice it was controlled by the capable hands of Sarah, her mother and her sisters. Before his marriage to Margaret Fell, George Fox had taken pains to ascertain the views of her children to the proposed marriage: he was particularly anxious that he should not be thought to be benefiting financially:

> When the rest of her daughters were come, I asked both them and her sons in law 'if they had anything against it or for it?' and they all severally expressed their satisfaction with it ... Whereupon I asked them, 'Whether, if their mother married, they should not lose by it?' ... I told them 'I was plain, and would have all things done plainly: for I sought not any outward advantage to myself' (Fox, 1765, p. 412).

For this family, membership of the Society of Friends reflected both a recognition of the importance of using money in a way that reflected moral values, and a concern for the equality of men and women. In exploring the relationship between ideas about gender equality and norms about the control and allocation of money, the example of the seventeenth century Quakers is interesting. At a time when the subordination of women was expressed in, and reinforced by, their financial dependence, the Quakers provide an alternative model, and one which provoked considerable disapproval from their contemporaries.

At about the same period, but in the south-east of England, another woman was succeeding in maintaining control of her property, again through the help of the Society of Friends. Mary Pennington's autobiography describes how her husband lost not only all his money but much of hers as well, so that they were evicted from their house. Mary, however, owned some land in Kent, and in 1654 it was suggested to her that she should sell this and build a new house for the family. The problem was that under common law a wife's money could be seized by her husband's creditors. The solution described in her autobiography is an early example of the use of a trust to protect the interests of a married woman against the provisions of the common law.

> I requested of my husband that seeing he had lost all, and the children had no provision but my estate, and that we were so tossed about and had no dwelling place for ourselves nor our children, I might build some little thing for them. My husband was averse to building, but I weighing that I could part with my land and buy a place with the money, and put it in condition for us and them, and he not be troubled with the building; that it should be made over to friends for me and the children (Pennington, 1848, p. 16).

It is interesting to see that, though Mary Pennington felt it necessary to ask her husband's permission, she nevertheless went ahead with building her house despite his aversion to the project.

On smaller farms and peasant holdings the typical pattern was for financial management to be divided between husband and wife, though the husband might have overall control. The effect was to produce an economy in which typically women and children provided for daily living expenses on a cash basis, while the men handled the stock or field crops and used the income from that source to pay bills for rent, replacement stock, farm labour and so on (Jensen, 1980; Malcolmson, 1981; Wrightson, 1982). The economic partnership between husband and wife, and the importance of mutual trust, were set out by Fitzherbert in his *Book of Husbandry*:

> It is a wyves occupation ... to go or ride to the market, to sel butter, chese, mylke, egges, chekyns, capons, hennes, pygges, gese, and all manner of cornes. And also to bye all maner of necessarye thynges belongynge to the houssholde, and to make a trewe rekenynge and a-compte to her housbande, what she hath payed. And yf the housbande go to the market to bye or sell, as they ofte do, he than to shewe his wife in lyke maner (Fitzherbert, 1534, p. 97).

It must be remembered, however, that the things which had to be bought in the market for such a household were relatively few by modern standards. Fitzherbert lists among the wife's occupations not only keeping the house clean and preparing meals for her husband and children, but also milking the cows, making cheese and butter, feeding the calves, pigs and hens, brewing, cultivating the vegetable garden, growing flax, spinning both flax and wool, and finally making all the clothes and linen for the household. With so much domestic production the sums to be expended at the market were relatively small. In these circumstances managing money might be a less significant measure of a wife's power within marriage than the skills and knowledge which she brought to the joint venture of running the farm.

The pattern for pre-industrial England was complicated. In general it seems that the more resources a household owned, the more likely it was that that control would be in male hands. Wives tended to pay for domestic expenditure for the household's daily needs, either out of an allowance received from the male head of household or out of their own production for sale. Where capital was concerned, or where there was a surplus of income over and above the daily needs of the household, management was likely to be in male hands. This reflected the fact that legally all the wife's income belonged to the husband and her land was under his control. However, particular circumstances could modify this pattern. In the early Middle Ages, before the codification of the common law, many women continued to own and manage their own property, as Eleanor Countess of Leicester had done. Even after the common law gave control of a wife's property into the hands of her husband, some wives could be found running the financial affairs of the household, particularly if, as in the case of Sarah Fell and her mother, there was ideological support for financial equality between the sexes.

On small farms, in shops and craft workshops, the roles of husband and wife were closely integrated, and the economic contribution of wives was beyond doubt. As Thomas Tusser put it, in a much quoted phrase: 'husbandrie weepeth, where huswiferie sleepeth' (Tusser, 1562, sig. S2.). However, the economic partnership was looser in the growing proportion of households whose dependence on wages forced the husband to work away from home. Among professional men the domestic sphere was often completely divorced from the world of work and the wife's economic role appeared to be that of managing consumption rather than contributing income. Houlbrooke contrasted the small farmer and his wife, whose time was spent together toiling in a shared enterprise, with a bureaucrat like Samuel Pepys whose wife was the companion of his leisure hours and whose office and home were separate worlds (Houlbrooke, 1984).

This book is concerned with the allocation of money within marriage and it is not possible to go in detail into the complications of the property settlements which occurred immediately before many marriages or after the death of parent or spouse. Death was one point at which property passed between generations and between the sexes. Typically sons inherited land, while daughters inherited money or an annuity; a daughter's inheritance could be used by her husband to pay his debts, or to add to his land holding, if it was not protected by a trust (Chaytor, 1980; Clay, 1968; Howell, 1976; Vann, 1979). Few married women made wills, partly because few had property to bequeath and partly because none could make a will without the consent of her husband. However, many women inherited from their husbands at the time of death and widows were the only women who were likely to own substantial amounts of property in their own right. Even the property of widows, however, was often subject to male control. A bewildering variety of local arrangements affected the financial position of widows, often with penalties if the widow married again or took a lover (Houlbrooke, 1984; Thompson, 1976).

Marriage was the time when an affluent father might settle money on a daughter, in trust for her and her children. The use of trusts was increasingly common from the seventeenth century; normally trusts were set up by fathers, though some husbands endowed their wives with an independent income by means of a marriage settlement (Houlbrooke, 1984, p. 100). At least one husband, Sir John Guise, bitterly resented the use of trusts to give wives a measure of financial independence, complaining that they originated in the 'folly of parents and the distrust of wives' and that they diminished 'the dignity and authority of a husband' (Davies, 1917, p. 152).

Marriage also marked the point at which land or money might be transferred from one family to another. Among better off families, the 'bride's portion' was a contribution from her family to his. It might take the form of land or cash, but if it was the latter the marriage settlement was likely to require the purchase of estates which were to descend with the patrimony (Chaytor, 1980; Bonfield, 1979). Though these flows of money took place through the medium of women, they were essentially flows between men, and as such were a crucial part of the process by which wealth became concentrated in the hands of particular individuals and families. Historians have documented the contribution which marriage settlements made to the rise of the great estates in the seventeenth and eighteenth centuries (Bonfield, 1979 and 1983; Broad, 1979; Clay 1968; Habbakuk, 1950).

The rise of great estates, and the creation of substantial concentrations of wealth, paved the way for the coming of the Industrial Revolution and for the profound economic and social changes which were to affect every aspect of British society. The growth of the business enterprise was associated with the removal of commercial and industrial activity from the home, and with the separation of business from domestic accounts; the slow and complex processes involved in this separation have been brilliantly documented by Davidoff and Hall (1987). The next section will be concerned with the ways in which these changes affected the control and allocation of money within the family and financial relationships between husband and wife.

The nineteenth and early twentieth centuries

The nineteenth century saw the growth of the great industrial cities and the development of an urban, wage earning proletariat and of a bourgeoisie which included clerks and shopkeepers, civil servants and professionals, as well as the owners of industrial and commercial enterprises of every size. In 1851 Britain became the first country in the history of the world in which a majority of the population lived in towns and cities. What did these changes mean for the financial arrangements of married couples? The nearer we come to the present day, the more plentiful do sources of evidence become. Increasing literacy meant that more people, from a wider social spectrum, felt able to write their personal life histories; the work of the first social scientists produced surveys of how people, and especially poorer people, lived their lives; and the development of oral history techniques opened the way to a rich source of data.

Throughout the nineteenth century large numbers of household manuals were published, with the explicit aim of assisting wives to manage the domestic economy more efficiently. The style of life portrayed in these manuals suggests that they were aimed at middle class families, and they tend to assume that the wife will be given a housekeeping allowance by her husband, or that he will pay the bills for goods which she has ordered (Beeton, 1861; Branca, 1976; Ellis, 1846; Walsh, 1857; Warren, 1864). By the middle of the century ruled and printed books were being sold specifically for the keeping of household accounts. Household manuals gave examples of 'typical' budgets for different income levels and their popularity suggests that many middle class wives did experience problems in managing the family finances. At the time this was attributed to inefficiency and extravagance on the part of wives, but it has been suggested that problems with finances were more likely to be a product of an imbalance between household income and the rising expectations of the Victorian middle class, the first real consumer society in the world (Branca, 1976).

Certainly the domestic division of labour gave to the wife the job of purchasing food, whether she went to the shops herself or had the goods delivered to the house. She may have paid in cash, but it seems likely that many households kept an account with each of the shopkeepers, who presented their bills at the end of every month. Whatever method the household adopted, the wife was seen as her husband's agent, responsible to him for the administration of his money. Mrs Beeton set out the duties of the mistress in this respect:

> A housekeeping account-book should invariably be kept, and kept punctually and precisely. The plan for keeping household accounts, which we should recommend, would be to make an entry, that is, write down into a daily diary every amount paid on that particular day, be it ever so small; then, at the end of the month, let these various payments be ranged under the specific heads of Butcher, Baker, *etc*; and thus will be seen the proportions paid to each tradesman, and any one month's expenses may be contrasted with another (Beeton, 1861, p. 6).

That the wife was acting as her husband's agent, rather than in her own right, can be seen from a rather melodramatic *Times* leader on the dangers which would flow from giving married women control of their own money:

> How are the expenses of a family to be divided? Commonly, a wife goes to market rather than the husband; that is she and not he, actually contracts debts with the butcher and baker. If she in future is to be personally liable for these debts – liable that is to be carried away from her children – would that be any gain to the sex? Marriage, it was observed, would on these terms, be not what it is now, but a kind of partnership: nobody sees better than Mr Mill that this proposal sets us on a slope of change. Where are we to stop? (*The Times*, 12 June 1868, p. 9).

'Mr Mill' refers, of course, to John Stuart Mill, whose book setting out the links between the subordination of women and the financial dependence of women within marriage was to be published in the following year (Mill, 1869).

How much housekeeping money did Victorian wives receive? What proportion of the husband's income was managed by his wife? The answer depends on the size of the total income: in general it seems that the lower the household income the larger was the proportion managed by the wife. A study of household incomes, based on tax returns and published in 1868, suggested that an income of £100–300 represented the lowest figure upon which a middle class life style could be maintained (Baxter, 1868). At about the same time 'typical' budgets were being published by Walsh (1857, p. 677). Out of a budget of £150 no less than £79 went on food and drink; rent and taxes amounted to £17.10.0d., the servant's wages to £10, and the rest was earmarked for washing, chandlery, clothing, illness and amusements. So it seems that at least half the household income was managed by the wife among the lower middle class, the level at which only one servant could be afforded.

A specific example of life at this level comes from the autobiography of Molly Vivian Hughes, who married in 1897. She was a teacher at Bedford College who gave up her job to marry Arthur Hughes, a young barrister. Their first home was in a flat near Portobello Lane in London and they had one servant called Emma. Molly Vivian Hughes wrote:

> Most newly married women have the same difficulties to meet: servants or the lack of them; finding good provision shops; keeping expenditure down ... Shopping in the lane brought my accounts down nicely, and I kept them rigidly, noting every item, such as 'parsley ½d. Everything was paid for by me except coal and Emma's wages, and I received thirty shillings from Arthur each Monday morning, frequently having four or five shillings in hand against unforeseens of the following week (Hughes, 1946, p. 536).

At other points in the autobiography it is clear that Arthur Hughes also paid for the flat and for his own clothes.

In general, however, contemporary published material says little about the details of Victorian family finances. In one middle class autobiography after another, each one packed with details about the people close to the writer, about the events of the day, about holidays, political debates, fashions, charitable work, novels and so on, there is a notable lack of comment about the way family finances were organised, just as there is little reference to sexual relationships. Both were clearly regarded as extremely private. It may be no accident that the nineteenth century was a period in which a high regard was paid to the privacy of the home, privacy which was often protective of the husband's domination over other members of the household, as Davidoff *et al.* have demonstrated (1976). Few middle class wives earned in their own right: even though some might have had money settled on them in the form of trusts, most were completely dependent on their husbands for the maintenance of their everyday standard of living. This meant that in most middle class households either the wife received an allowance to pay for household expenses and for her own needs, or else her husband paid the bills and she had little or no money for her own use. In either case the amount of money which a wife received must have been a crucial factor in determining the extent to which she could exercise autonomy in her own life. If wives had been in the habit of comparing notes about how much money they received from their husbands this would surely have led to a questioning of male authority. The lack of evidence about housekeeping money may be a measure of how powerful that authority was, an example of the way in which power can take the form of simply keeping a topic off the agenda (Lukes, 1974; see also Wohl, 1978).

Much more information is available about the working class in the nineteenth and early twentieth centuries. Members of the middle classes, who would probably have been outraged had a stranger called at the house to enquire into the details of their own family finances, felt no scruples about investigating the financial problems of the poor. In addition, working class autobiographies, and the memories collected by oral historians, make it clear that the management of family income was an important issue, at least for women, and was a topic of conversation and comment in a way that it never was among the middle class. Most of the evidence suggests that in working class households wives were largely responsible for managing family finances. However, there were many different variations on the typical pattern, reflecting not only income levels, but also the characteristics of particular individuals and families, the cultural norms of particular areas, the ways in which wages were paid and a variety of other variables.

One problem is to know where the divide came between those households where the wife handled all or almost all the money, and those where she received an allowance from a husband who retained a substantial part of his earnings. Loane has suggested that in 1909 an income of 40 shillings a week was the point below which the wife generally had the management of all the wages except the husband's pocket money (Loane, 1909). Work on middle class incomes has suggested that £300 was the minimum for a secure middle class household, though a semblance of a middle class life style could be achieved on an income as low as £100 per year (Banks, 1954; Branca, 1976). This figure is, of course, the same as the 40 shillings per week quoted by Loane, so it seems likely that this was indeed a crucial dividing point. Corroborative evidence comes from the study of Yorkshire steelworkers carried out by Lady Bell (1911). This suggested that housekeeping allowances were more common among workers earning over 40 shillings per week. She cited one man whose wages were nearly £3 per week, who always put 30 shillings into one pocket for his wife: he said 'Whatever happens, I put 30s. in here for her, and she needn't mind what is in the other one.' (Bell, 1911, p. 122). Another man earned 50 to 68 shillings per week and Bell commented 'He gives his wife 28s. to keep house on, out of which she pays his sick club ... What is done with the balance of her husband's wages is not stated.' (Bell, 1911, p. 123).

Evidence that working class wives typically managed all, or almost all, of the family income comes from many parts of the country: London (Loane, 1905 and 1909; Pember Reeves, 1914; Ross, 1982); north-west England (Roberts, 1984); north-east England (Mourby, 1983); Yorkshire (Bell, 1911; Burnett, 1974; John, 1982); Oxfordshire (Thompson, 1945). Some historians have argued that among the Victorian working class husband and wife should be seen as partners, with wives gaining self-esteem from their role as family financial manager (Roberts, 1984). Loane, who was a nurse working in the East End of London, suggested that control of money extended the wife's sphere of influence into every part of family life:

> Money matters are left entirely to the wife; it is she who decides whether an increased rent can be paid or an article of furniture bought, whether a boy shall be apprenticed or must take what work he can find, and what insurance clubs, *etc.* shall be joined. The custom of leaving the management of money to the wife is so deeply rooted, that children always speak of the family income as belonging entirely to her, and will constantly tell you: 'Mother has to pay so and so for rent'; 'Mother is going to try and afford Father this or that'; 'Mother isn't going to let Father work for Mr — any more, she says the wages isn't worth the hours' (Loane, 1905, p. 12).

On the other hand, there is rather more evidence for the acceptance by both men and women of the subordination of wives within marriage. A wife was expected to cope as best she could with what her husband was able to earn, or rather with what he chose to give her, and he was often unwilling to share the burden of making ends meet (Meacham, 1977; Taylor, 1977). Many husbands kept their wives in ignorance of how much they earned: among the steelworkers of Yorkshire one third of the women did not know what their husbands' wages were (Bell, 1911, p. 121). A study of family life in Lancashire, an area noted for female responsibility for the management of household finances, showed that many wives did not

know how much their husbands earned (Anderson, 1971, p. 210).
An interview with a Nottingham woman who was born in 1911
shows the way in which the superiority of men within the home was
an accepted fact, and what this implied for wives:

Q. Did your father or mother control the money in the house?
R. All that he gave her – never gave her enough though, to live on.
Q. So they didn't run it together?
R. No, my dad had his – my dad gave me mam so much and that was it.
    I used to fetch it, so I know. He had a good wage then – on
    corporation – he got £4.5s. I used to have to go for the money
    because he'd never come home you know – and he used to give me
    £2 . . . he used to go out drinking and that – that's how life is – my
    mam had to suffer, that's why I don't blame women for fighting for
    their rights – cause my mam should have done. I mean, £2 to keep
    yourself and six children on (Taylor, 1977, p. 48).

One result of the wife's responsibility for family finances is that
the whole topic becomes invisible in many historical documents.
Accounts of the male world, written by men, are full of information
about the technicalities of particular jobs, about drinking habits,
working class hobbies, and so on, but there is usually little about
how money is managed once it is earned. It is difficult to substantiate
this point, since in any specific context the fact that something is not
mentioned is hardly of interest. However, one example of the
invisibility of women's financial management comes in Bourne's
record of his talks with a Surrey peasant. This is a detailed account
of rural life in the late nineteenth century; the only comment made
on the subject of money management is:

I've worked wi' chaps not taking as much as me, and they bin as well off
as I was. Whatever you earns, you lives up to it. Very often, them as earns
the most money be wuss off than them as takes less (Bourne, 1901, p. 295).

Knowing the low level of agricultural wages at the time, all these
men, if they were married, would be looked after by wives who were
engaged in an exhausting struggle to make ends meet. Some would
have fewer mouths to feed and some would be better managers,
while others would be going hungry themselves in order to feed the
breadwinner, but there is no acknowledgement of any of this in
Talks with a Surrey Peasant. Similarly, Vincent's study of nineteenth
century working class autobiographies contained almost nothing

about how families organised their money beyond the statement that, 'The wife was in charge of the household budget and her efficiency, ingenuity and courage in a crisis were crucial to the economic survival of the family' (Vincent, 1981, p. 53). Vincent's study examined 142 autobiographies, of which only six were by women, so his data reflect a male view of the period; by contrast, in the accounts of working class life now being collected from women by oral historians, managing the family budget is a central concern.

The amount the husband spent on himself had a crucial impact on the standard of living of the rest of the family. One characteristic of a 'good' husband was that he should retain as small a sum as possible. Many investigators commented that it was impossible for a family to be adequately fed and clothed on the average working class wage if any members of the family spent money on alcohol or gambling (Pember Reeves, 1914; Roberts, 1977 and 1984; Rowntree, 1901; Treble, 1979). Some wives drank and gambled, but far more often it was the husband who escaped to the pub from the drudgery of work and the drabness and overcrowding of home. 'Secondary poverty' was the term used by Rowntree to describe the situation in which a family's total income could have been sufficient for its needs had not a portion of that income been absorbed by other expenditure, either useful or wasteful. Rowntree identified spending on alcohol, usually by the husband, as the main cause of secondary poverty, estimating that about one sixth of a working class family's income, on average, was spent in this way, representing an average of 31 pints of beer per week (Rowntree, 1901). The term 'secondary poverty' has served to minimise the seriousness of a condition which may have felt worse than 'primary poverty' to the women who experienced the uncertainty of not knowing how much money they would have to feed the family, and the bitterness of seeing children go hungry unnecessarily. In recalling a working class childhood, many people remember the weekly anxiety over whether father would return home with his wage packet or whether a child would have to be sent to retrieve what was left. Lilian Westall, who became a parlour maid, described how

The other day I went back to the King's Cross area in London. I walked along the Pentonville Road and looked at some of the pubs that had been there sixty years ago, and I was back in my childhood. I saw the same swing doors that I had pushed open and remembered the noise that had gushed out; remembered running from pub to pub, long skirts flapping, a skinny, breathless, frightened thirteen year old, looking for my father, trying to get him to come home before he spent all his pay. Usually I failed. There were many times when most of his money had gone by Saturday night (Burnett, 1974, p. 215).

The custom of paying wages in pubs was one cause of excessive spending on alcohol. Often the wages of three or four men would be paid in a lump sum, as a five pound note or a number of sovereigns, and the men were expected to get this changed into smaller coins so that each could take his share. An old potter from Tunstall described his experience of a publican who refused to give change unless each customer bought at least a hot roll and cheese, and who often delayed paying the money in full till drinking had begun in earnest:

> Not until he was assured of a fair return for his 'change', or until his adult customers were settled for a night's booze, did he bring out the change . . . When all were paid the women and boys were sent home, the night's booze properly set in, and toward ten o'clock poor wretched women would appear and entreat their husbands to go home. When this failed they pleaded for money, as they had not a penny with which to pay the week's bills or to provide for the morrow (Burnett, 1974, p. 303).

In 1842 it was made illegal to pay miners in this way, but it was not till 1883 that it became illegal to pay any workmen in a public house (Hunt, 1981).

Not only did husbands receive pocket money in a way that wives rarely did, but they also received a larger share of the resources devoted to the family. Both in his diet, and in terms of health care if he became ill, the breadwinner was a privileged member of the household. Men were more likely to have their health insured and to receive prompt and adequate medical attention. As Hunt pointed out, this uneven distribution of income within the family was beneficial to productivity at the workplace but it was obviously detrimental to the health of wives and children (Hunt, 1981, p. 123).

There is ample evidence that nineteenth century working class women had poorer diets than men, and that this was reflected in their health (Anderson, 1971; Booth, 1903; Llewelyn Davies, 1915; Oddy, 1970; Oren, 1974; Thane, 1978). Perhaps the most detailed evidence of this comes from a nutritional study conducted by Dr T. Oliver (1895). Investigating diets in Newcastle-on-Tyne, he showed that the mean calorie intake was 3300 kilocalories for men and 1870 kilocalories for women. The consumption of fats by men was three times the consumption by women, while men consumed twice as much protein as did women. Essentially, the women's daily diet was based on bread and tea, while almost all the men consumed a main meal of meat, bacon or fish, with potatoes (Oliver, 1895).

Dietary inequalities between men and women were reflected in mortality rates. Late twentieth century mortality rates are higher for men than women at every age, reflecting the lower life expectancy of men. However, in the mid-nineteenth century mortality rates for the age group from ten to 34 were higher for women than for men. This difference has been attributed to the dangers of childbirth and also to the prevalence of tuberculosis, both of which were exacerbated by a diet which was poorer than that of men in terms of quantity and quality. Wives went short of food in order to feed their husbands, while daughters were deemed to need less food, and less nutritious food, than sons (Johansson, 1977).

Between 1890 and 1914 an increase in the wage rates of skilled men meant that some surplus became available over and above the subsistence needs of the family. It seems likely that as wages rose many men retained the surplus and abandoned the traditional pattern of turning most of their income over to their wives for family use. Observers who compared British working class couples with their counterparts in France and Germany noted that there were no reports from the latter of women sacrificing their own diet in order to keep their husbands happy, as was common among the British working class (Stearns, 1972, p. 119). It is interesting to speculate about the extent to which these differences reflected, on the one hand, the tradition of community property in marriage, and, on the other hand, the more individual property régime developed by the British legal system.

These two chapters have explored the historical evidence about patterns of allocation of money within marriage. Legally, from the thirteenth to the nineteenth centuries, the money coming to both husband and wife was *controlled* by the husband: in this the law reflected an idea about the subordination of women within marriage which was accepted by both men and women. In practice, wives sometimes *managed* substantial areas of family finances. While in general it was among the poorer families that wives had the greater financial responsibility, this pattern was not universal. In time of war when husbands were absent, in sub-cultures which valued equality between the sexes, where a trust protected the inheritance of a wife, or where an individual husband had a high regard for his wife's financial skills, a wife might take more part in managing family finances. However, the fact that the legal position was not seriously questioned until the mid-nineteenth century suggests a high degree of acceptance for the idea of male control of finance, even if some management was delegated to women. Financial dependency was a cornerstone in a complicated social, ideological and economic structure which maintained the subordination of wives within marriage and the acceptance on the part of wives that the needs of husband and children should take precedence over their own needs.

4

Background to the study

The historical evidence suggested that in the past couples have organised their money in a variety of different ways. What are the patterns in late twentieth century Britain? The following chapters set out to answer this question, drawing evidence from the results of a number of different empirical surveys, some of which were carried out by social scientists exploring a variety of different issues, while others were carried out by market research firms investigating markets for particular products. At the heart of the book is the empirical study which I carried out myself in order to investigate the control and allocation of money within families in Britain in the late twentieth century. This chapter sets out the problems which the study was attempting to explore, discusses some of the recent research on which I drew in developing my ideas, and outlines the study itself.

The study aimed to investigate a number of different but related hypotheses. The hypotheses derived from personal experience, from previous research, and from contemporary and historical sources; many have already been set out, explicitly or implicitly, in chapters 2 and 3. The first and most fundamental hypothesis was that couples do organise their money in significantly different ways, and that it is possible to devise a typology, or typologies, of allocative systems. The historical evidence provided ample support for this hypothesis. Clearly there were important differences between the independent management of money exemplified by the Earl and Countess of Leicester in the late thirteenth century and the shared financial management of couples who farmed the small peasant holdings of pre-industrial England. Similarly, there were great contrasts

46

between the extreme financial dependence of some nineteenth century middle class wives and the crushing financial responsibility of many working class women of the same period.

A second set of hypotheses derived from the argument that the allocative systems adopted by couples are related to other aspects of their lives, such as the level of income of the household, whether both, or one or neither partner is in paid employment, and so on. The historical evidence suggested that the higher the household income, the more likely it was that overall control would be in the hands of the husband; similarly, the higher the household income, the larger would be the proportion managed by the husband. The historical evidence also suggested that when wives earned in their own right, or when they were producers of goods for sale, such as eggs and butter, wool and cloth, then they were likely to have more say in financial management. So the study was concerned not just with documenting existing patterns of allocation, but also with analysing the economic forces which shape these patterns and which lead to changes over time.

However, material conditions alone do not provide complete explanations for phenomena as complex as those with which we are concerned. As the historical evidence suggested, particular ideologies can shape human relations in profound ways. Thus, the complex web of ideology supporting male dominance and female subordination, which has been described as patriarchy, has been of central importance in structuring patterns of allocation of money within marriage; the fact that patriarchal ideologies have been given greater legitimation by being incorporated into statute and case law has added to their strength and persistence. On the other hand there are ideologies which stress equality between men and women within marriage. So a third set of hypotheses was concerned with the ways in which financial arrangements within a marriage can serve as evidence of more fundamental social processes. Using money as tracer, it might be possible to explore the relative significance of material conditions, on the one hand, and ideology on the other hand, as determinants of the very different ways in which men and women experience marriage. Does the allocative system adopted by a couple more closely reflect the economic position of the household or the norms and values held by either or both partners?

This line of thought was developed into a set of hypotheses concerned with the notion of dependence. It seemed likely that financial inequality would be translated into, and would reflect, other sorts of inequality. Evidence from the nineteenth century suggested the existence of a circular process in which middle class wives, because of their financial dependence, were conventionally portrayed as weak, vulnerable and lacking in worldly experience; being attributed with these qualities made wives appear to be unsuited to the management of large sums of money, so reinforcing their financial dependence. A related set of assumptions concerned the responsibility of wives for child care and domestic work and so the appropriateness of a 'family wage' which would enable a male breadwinner to support his dependent wife and children. One aim of the study was to explore the notion of dependence as it exists in Britain today. Do husbands still see themselves as responsible for providing the family wage and if so, what does this imply for the earnings of wives? What rewards are attached to being an earner, and is receiving earned money different from receiving social security? Is being a breadwinner a burden or a privilege, an unwelcome responsibility or a source of power? Answers to these questions could add both to our understanding of marriage and to our knowledge about the nature of economic life.

The study also offered an opportunity to investigate a number of hypotheses developed by sociologists of marriage and the family. For example, it has been argued that power within marriage is directly related to the control of financial resources: the higher the proportion of the household's income which an individual contributes, the greater will be that person's power in marital decision-making. However, this hypothesis relates to money as it enters the household. Within the household money may remain in the control of the spouse who earned it, or may be passed to the other partner. Does power pass with the money or does it remain with the earning partner? What is the relationship between different sorts of power, from the power to decide how a family's money should be organised to the power over particular spending decisions? Another set of theoretical issues has revolved around the nature of marriage and of gender roles within it. For example, one debate has been concerned with the rather different experience of men and women within marriage. How different are the accounts which husbands and wives give of their financial arrangements? It is not appropriate to develop these and similar debates until they can be explored more fully in later chapters. At this stage the aim has been to give a brief review of some of the theoretical issues which the study aimed to tackle, as an introduction to a discussion of previous empirical work on the topic and a description of the study which forms the basis of this book.

Classifications and concepts

Inevitably an empirical study of this sort builds on the work of previous researchers. As we have seen, there have been many who have in passing presented information about how married couples organised their finances, but few for whom it was a central issue. In this section we consider the work of some of those who have investigated the allocation of money in a more systematic way. How did they classify systems of allocation of money? What were the bases of their conceptual frameworks?

There have been a number of attempts to develop typologies of financial arrangements. One of the earliest was by Zweig, in his study of male workers in Sheffield, Workington, Luton, Erdington and Mitcham (Zweig, 1961). He asked respondents whether they gave their wives a housekeeping allowance or not, whether the sum was fixed or variable, and whether it had to cover all bills including the rent. The nature of the sample and the wording of the question is likely to have biased the results. Only men were interviewed, though their wives might have given different answers. Since the initial focus of the series of questions was on the paying of housekeeping money, it is perhaps not surprising that the regular and fixed allowance was the most common pattern.

The arrangements documented by Zweig fell into eight different categories:

1. The regular and fixed housekeeping allowance. This covered food and some bills and the system was used by 52 per cent of the men.

2. The variable housekeeping allowance covered the same items as the previous system, but the amount handed from husband to wife varied: 8 per cent of the men.

3. Housekeeping allowance for food only with all the bills paid by the husband: 9 per cent of the men.

4. The whole wage packet handed to the wife, with pocket money being returned by her to the husband: 10 per cent of the men.

5. The whole wage packet handed over after the husband had taken out his pocket money: 6 per cent of the men.

6. A percentage, such as four fifths or two thirds of earnings handed to the wife: 1 per cent of the men.

7. Wages placed in a drawer or kitty to which the wife has free access: 2 per cent of the men.

8. The pooling of earnings was described as a very popular arrangement with young couples: it was used by 12 per cent of the men.

Finally, Zweig mentioned what he called 'a very peculiar arrangement' which a respondent described as 'what she makes is hers, what I make is mine': as we shall see, since Zweig identified it in 1961, this 'peculiar arrangement' has become much more common, especially among young, professional couples in the south-east of England.

Zweig's typology was based on answers from men and reflects the male earner's perspective on this issue, in that distinctions between types of allocative system were based on the amounts handed from husband to wife and on variations from week to week. In types 1, 2, 3 and 6 a part of the husband's wage packet was handed over, in the form of an allowance to the wife, while the remainder was retained by him for use as his pocket money and to pay one or more household bills. In types 4 and 5 the whole wage packet was handed over, either before or after the husband's pocket money was taken out. In types 7 and 8 the husband's wage packet was shared with his wife and Zweig commented that this arrangement was particularly common when both partners were earning. To summarise, in this sample of 337 men living in the south and centre of England in 1958, 16 per cent of men gave their whole wage to their wives, 70 per cent gave their wives an allowance and 14 per cent pooled their earnings. This will be important evidence when we look at how patterns of allocation of money have changed over time.

In her study of 84 working class families in Edinburgh, carried out in 1969, Gray drew on Zweig's work (Gray, 1974 and 1979). However, her account of the family as an economic unit was as much concerned with spending as with earning, and her analysis of allocation patterns was much more processual. Her study explored the relationships between the family's budgeting system, its expenditure pattern and the amount of overtime worked by husbands. It showed that husbands who handed their whole wage packet over to their wives were less likely to do overtime than those who handed over a specific amount and retained the remainder of their earnings. A similar pattern was found among teenagers in two other studies carried out in the 1960s. These showed that teenagers who handed over all their earnings to their mothers, retaining only a fixed sum for pocket money, were less likely to do overtime than those who handed over a fixed sum for board and lodging and kept the rest to spend as they chose (Millward, 1968; Shimmin, 1962).

Gray made a distinction between the 'housekeeping allowance' and 'collective expenditure'. The former term was used to refer to the money given by the husband to the wife; the latter term referred to all those items bought with this money, with money retained by him but spent on behalf of the family and with money earned by the wife. Gray classified allocation systems according to 'the proportion of collective expenditure made out of the husband's retentions' (Gray, 1974, p. 135). She made a distinction between systems where the husband had responsibility for one or more major items of collective expenditure, such as rent, fuel or furniture, which she called 'System A', and those where he had little or no responsibility for collective expenditure, which she called 'System B'. System A was used by 45 per cent of the families and was more common among owner-occupiers and couples with higher incomes. It was similar to the allowance system, described by Zweig as types 1, 2, 3 and 6. System B was used by 53 per cent of the families and was more common among low income couples, especially if they came from traditional backgrounds such as mining, fishing or farming. It was similar to the whole wage system identified by Zweig as types 4 and 5 (Zweig, 1961). Gray also interviewed two couples who pooled their earnings, but did not include them in the analysis of budgeting systems, presumably because they seemed so unusual.

Gray suggested that previous studies had focused on the housekeeping allowance, while ignoring the husband's other contributions to collective expenditure. She argued that among working class families in the late 1960s budgeting was much less of a female responsibility that had been believed in the 1950s and earlier. Her study showed that the husband's contribution to collective expenditure increased at higher income levels and where there were more children. However, she did not investigate whether the contribution made by a husband to collective expenditure increased in direct proportion to his earnings.

This issue was addressed by MacLeod in an important but unpublished study carried out in Newcastle-on-Tyne in the late 1960s (MacLeod, 1977). He showed that as the net income of the husband increased there was a marked tendency for the proportion paid over as the housekeeping allowance to fall. Among husbands who gave a housekeeping allowance, the majority gave between 70 and 50 per cent. However, the proportion giving less than 70 per cent of their income fell to 22 per cent among the lowest earners and rose to 86 per cent among the highest earners (MacLeod, 1977, p. 152).

MacLeod divided systems of money management into two types, which he called 'joint management' and 'lump sum'. In practice joint management might mean either that the couple shared management of the income or that management was the responsibility of the wife. MacLeod argued that the difference was not important since in both cases the couple had made the joint decision that the whole of the income of the husband, or of husband and wife, was their common concern:

> The essential point was that the partners, and particularly the husband, did not withhold from the other partner any control over the income received. The most common practical result of this situation was that the wife actually assumed the management of the income but the common characteristic of both types of arrangement was that the couple exercised joint control over the income (MacLeod, 1977, p. 143).

The distinction between management and control is an important aspect of financial arrangements and one to which we shall return.

MacLeod did not refer to the work of Zweig or Gray, but the 'joint management' system which he described was similar to the 'whole wage system' identified by Zweig and to the 'System B' described by Gray, though in MacLeod's typology the category included couples who pooled their money and shared in its management. However, as we have seen, pooling couples were rare in Zweig and Gray's studies, and MacLeod also presented this as an unusual system (Zweig, 1961; Gray, 1974; MacLeod, 1977). 'Joint management' was the system adopted by 39 per cent of the 451 couples interviewed by MacLeod, while in 61 per cent of couples the husband gave his wife a 'lump sum'.

MacLeod's 'lump sum' was similar to the 'allowance system' identified by Zweig and to the 'System A' described by Gray. However, MacLeod saw the issue of control as central. He distinguished between his two systems on this basis:

> In one system the partners exercised common control over the whole income and in the other the husband, by virtue of his initial control over his earnings, reserved for himself the management of a part and in extreme cases, the whole, of his income (MacLeod, 1977, p. 143).

MacLeod went on to argue that the 'lump sum' arrangement was part of the process by which the husband maintained his superior authority within the marriage. He suggested that it was common for the husband, because he was the breadwinner for the family, to assume that by virtue of his having earned the income, he should retain overall control of the money, while delegating the management of a part of it to the housekeeping wife. It was significant that among husbands who were sick or unemployed a number stated that they made over the whole of their income when they were receiving social security benefits, but changed the arrangement to a lump sum housekeeping allowance when they were working. Wives who received a lump sum for housekeeping often referred to this as their 'wage', as though their relationship to the breadwinner resembled that of an employee to an employer.

Zweig and Gray were important influences on my own early attempt to develop a typology of allocative systems (Pahl, 1980). However, a more significant influence was Edwards, who published her study of 50 Australian couples in 1981. She emphasised the distinction between management and control in a way reminiscent of MacLeod:

> 'Management' of finance is akin to the implementation functions performed within any enterprise – the carrying out of decisions which have already been made. The manager of family finances would handle family money and would make the actual payments. However, s/he may not in fact have a major role in financial decision-making and might be given directions from other family members as to what to buy. 'Control' refers more to the decision-making aspect of family finances. It is akin to the policy-making functions of any enterprise (Edwards, 1981, p. 4).

Edwards suggested that 'management is more a matter of facts; control more a matter of perception' (Edwards, 1981, p. 26). She noted a number of criteria which might be used to determine where control lay. These included the freedom which each partner had to spend money on themselves, the extent to which husband and wife were expected to justify expenditure to each other, whether either could spend on items of which the other disapproved, and who had the final say on major purchases.

Out of her 50 couples Edwards identified three examples of wife control, 20 of husband control and 27 of joint control. She concluded that lower income husbands tended to say that they had a dominant role in financial decision-making, even when by the criteria set out above financial control appeared to be shared. By contrast, higher income husbands tended to say that there was more of an egalitarian relationship even if in fact the husband had overall control of finances. Finally, some women said that their husbands had financial control, when in reality, it was they who were abdicating from joint control. These results raise the question of whether control can be defined objectively, and of the relationship between objective and subjective perception.

When she turned from control to management, Edwards drew on the typologies developed by earlier researchers, but adapted some of the classifications to fit in with her emphasis on the management of family finances. She outlined four systems, which she described as 'wife management', 'husband management', 'joint management' and 'independent management'. She sub-divided the whole wage system into two, depending on whether it was managed by the wife or by the husband. Whole wage systems managed by the wife were designated 'wife management'. Whole wage systems managed by the husband were grouped with systems in which the husband gave his wife an allowance, retaining the rest of his income and paying at least one major bill: these were described as 'husband management'. The pooling of income, so that both partners had access to all or almost all the household income, and both had responsibility for paying bills, was designated 'shared management'. Finally, arrangements in which each partner had an income, neither had access to the other's income but each had responsibility for at least one major bill, were described as 'independent management'. Out of the 50 couples, Edwards identified 25 in which money was managed by the wife and seven by the husband; in seven cases management was shared and in

11 husband and wife managed their finances independently.

Though Edwards made links between money and power, as an economist this was not her main focus. Other feminist researchers have explored in more detail the ways in which patterns of allocation of money reflect and reinforce inequalities in power between husband and wife. Thus Whitehead, in a comparative analysis of the allocation of resources within households in West Africa and Britain pointed to the asymmetries in power which are reflected, for example, in the fact that personal spending money is taken for granted by men but is rare for women. She set out to deconstruct the household and to examine the processes by which individual household members gain access to, and control over, the resources which are available to the household as a whole. She used the phrase 'conjugal contract' to refer to the terms on which husbands and wives exchange goods, incomes and services, including labour, within the household. Her analysis drew attention to the conflicts of interest between husbands and wives which different forms of conjugal contract entail. She concluded by emphasising that 'despite ideology, the household is not a collectivity of mutually reciprocal interests' (Whitehead, 1981, p. 110).

Whitehead's emphasis on the inevitability of conflict within marriage is important, in that it recognises that the relationships between individuals within the family reflect their structural position outside the family. The conjugal contract grows out of the different economic and social positions of men and women and is shaped by ideologies about the nature of gender relationships.

Hunt explored the significance of ideology in her study of gender and class consciousness (Hunt, 1978 and 1980). She identified control of household finances as a crucial factor in marital power and suggested that the way in which a couple handled its money was a significant indicator of the nature of their relationship (Hunt, 1980, p. 37). Comparing couples where only one partner was employed with other couples where both were in employment, she showed how even when wives earned, their wages were still seen as secondary to those of the breadwinner. Thus the ideology of the male breadwinner and the female homemaker reinforced the practical realities of a situation in which wives, if they earned at all, typically earned less than husbands. Hunt argued that the structural and ideological situation of dependants leaves them with little or no choice but to accept the dominance of the breadwinner, should he want to exercise his power. In this model, power resides in earning/controlling, rather than in spending/managing.

Land's contribution to our understanding of this topic has been both empirical and conceptual. In her study of 86 large families in London she divided couples according to responsibility for expenditure. In 44 per cent of the families husband and wife were jointly responsible for household expenditure. However, more commonly the wife was responsible for most household expenditure, using a part of the husband's earnings in 32 per cent of cases and all his earnings in 24 per cent of cases. In these large families, many of whom lived on very low incomes, the money earned by wives was invariably used for housekeeping (Land, 1969, p. 65). Land's study demonstrated that, though wives played a major role in managing household finances, they were still likely to deprive themselves if resources were short. The constraints of a low income were not shared equally. Instead,

> Resources are allocated by reference to custom or tradition and the interests of some members of the family are sacrificed to the interests of others. In particular, it is noticeable that in many respects the mother of the family puts the needs of her husband and children before her own (Land, 1977, p. 174).

Land used empirical evidence to support the argument that the distribution of resources between men and women reflects their relative power: 'Men get a larger share of the resources because they have more power than women within the family' (Land, 1983, p. 66). She has gone on to explore the many ways in which social policies have had the effect of exacerbating inequalities within the family, by ignoring the differences in power between men and women and by making the assumption that the family is a unit and that the typical couple consists of an earning husband and a dependent wife (Land, 1983 and 1986). This issue will be discussed more fully in chapter 8.

In this section we have examined a number of different methods of classifying patterns of money management, and have identified some of the key concepts. We considered five different classification systems. Zweig's system was based on the proportion of the husband's income which was handed to the wife; Gray focused on the extent to which the husband retained responsibility for major bills; MacLeod distinguished between couples on the basis of who had overall control of money within the household; Edwards classified couples both by overall control and by responsibility for daily management; finally, Land divided her families according to the wife's access to household income and her responsibility for expenditure (Zweig, 1961; Gray, 1979; MacLeod, 1977; Edwards, 1981; Land, 1969). Thus, though it is possible to devise typologies of allocative systems, and though there is considerable overlap between them, it is important to recognise that the criteria upon which typologies are based vary widely. Some different methods of classifying allocative systems will be examined in chapter 5.

This section has also introduced some key concepts which will be explored in the chapters which follow. First, there is an important distinction to be made between *collective* and *individual* expenditure. Clearly there are some items, such as housing, fuel and basic food stuffs, which most households buy collectively, and in respect of which there can be little or no variation between the standards of living of different members of the household. At the other extreme there are items which are typically bought on an individual basis, such as cigarettes, clothes, and entertainment, and here there can be considerable variations in the standards of living of different people within the same household. These variations may, of course, reflect individual tastes, but they can also reflect access to income, whether earned or shared within the household. As we shall see, households differ between those within which the standards of living of all members are very similar and those within which large numbers of items are bought and consumed on an individual basis and there may be considerable inequalities.

Secondly, there is an important distinction between control and management. *Control* is mainly exercised at the point where money enters the household. It is concerned with decisions such as which allocative system should be adopted within the household, which spouse should have the final say on major financial decisions, and with the extent to which spouses have control over personal spending money of their own and access to joint money. *Management* is concerned with putting into operation the particular allocative system which the couple have adopted. Household expenditure takes place within a number of different categories, such as food, fuel, clothes, rent or mortgage, insurance, transport, leisure activities and so on. The management function can extend over all of these categories, or it may be confined to just one or two. In this book two typologies will be developed and used in the analysis. The first divides the couples into four categories according to their system of money management. The second divides them into four rather different categories according to overall control of finances.

The idea of the *conjugal contract* is also valuable. It is an ambiguous concept, bringing together as it does the notion of a freely agreed exchange with the reality of an exchange which takes place in a context of inequality between men and women, both within marriage and in the wider society. This inequality may be based on differential access to material resources or it may reflect ideologies about the nature of gender relationships.

In conceptualising flows of money within the household, it is useful to see variables such as age, sex, marital status and employment status as *filter points* which control an individual's access to household income; these variables also affect the extent to which any one individual plays a role as a controller, a manager, or a consumer of household resources. A child, for example, may have no control over the family finances, may manage only her own pocket money but yet be a privileged consumer. A non-earning wife who receives a housekeeping allowance from her husband may have little control over household income, while playing a major role as a manager; her husband's role as an earner and controller of income enables him to hand over the work of spending to someone who will protect his interests as a consumer. The filtering effects of age, sex, marital status and employment status may be seen more clearly in a cross-cultural context. In our society marriage typically marks the point at which a woman takes on responsibility for managing collective expenditure on behalf of a household, in contrast to other societies in which married people may remain in their parents' households and men are the main spenders (see examples in Dwyer and Bruce, 1988).

The study

A detailed discussion of the methods used in the study is given in appendix 1. At this stage my intention is simply to outline the objectives of the study, to describe how those objectives were tackled, and to give some indication of the strengths and weaknesses of the data presented in the chapters which follow.

The main aim of the study was to gain a better knowledge of

patterns of financial management within households and to investigate the significance of different allocative systems for individual members of households. I would have liked to have studied a variety of household types living in several different parts of Britain. However, time and money were both limited, so the research focused on married couples with at least one child under 16 and was carried out in three different parts of Kent. The study was concerned not only with documenting existing patterns of allocation of money but also with analysing the social and economic processes which shaped those patterns and which might lead to changes over time. I wanted to explore the extent to which patterns of allocation were related to other variables such as the level of a couple's income, their age and educational attainment, and whether both partners, one or neither was in employment.

Secondly, I aimed to investigate the relationships between patterns of allocation of money and other dimensions in the lives of husbands and wives, building on the work of previous researchers. It seemed that money might be used as a 'tracer' reflecting and reinforcing other aspects of marriage, such as deference and authority, dependence and independence. Could the distinction between control and management be identified empirically and what did it mean in practice? To what extent could analysis of financial arrangements lead to a better understanding of the conjugal contract and of the relative power of husband and wife?

Thirdly, I hoped that the study would contribute to relevant policy debates. Policy makers have notoriously treated the family, the household and the couple as economic units. This has been particularly true in the field of taxation and income maintenance, but similar assumptions have been apparent in statements by policy analysts writing about, for example, the problem of debt or the distribution of poverty. One aim of the study was to provide a body of data which would illuminate future policy decisions on these topics. Another aim was to investigate household spending patterns and the extent to which the control of money within the household affected responsibility for expenditure. This is important in developing a better understanding of the reasons why standards of living can vary within as well as between households.

Married, or as-married, couples with dependent children can be contacted in various different ways, but it seemed that health centre records offered the best means for getting access to a near-complete population of couples with children. Accordingly, children under 16, living with both parents, were identified from the age-sex registers held in three different health centres; from these a random sample was selected and approached with a request for an interview.

There were a number of problems with contacting the respondents. A relatively large proportion refused to be interviewed, so that the final response rate was only 52 per cent. The high refusal rate seemed to reflect partly the fact that money was defined as too private a topic for discussion with a stranger, and partly the fact that both husband and wife were to be interviewed. Many individuals who were willing to participate did not do so because their partners were reluctant or unwilling; men were more likely to refuse than women. The attitude of many refusing couples was summed up by one woman who said 'I wouldn't mind myself. But my husband doesn't want to do it. He says "What's our business is our business"'.

Carrying out the interviews took much longer than had been anticipated. A team of seven interviewers was specially trained to work on the project. They used structured questionnaires but were encouraged to note down verbatim comments by respondents when it seemed that this would illuminate particular replies. The interviewing took ten months to complete. This was largely because each separate interview required the presence of four people, two respondents and two interviewers, and so there were often long delays between contacting a couple and completing an interview with them. However, this rather time-consuming method was justified by the results. There were frequently wide discrepancies between the husband's and the wife's answers to the same question. The results made it clear that studies which use either husband or wife as respondent on behalf of the couple cannot make the assumption that this always represents the position of the spouse who was not interviewed.

Two aspects of the interviews gave cause for concern. One was the difficulty which many respondents found in answering some of the questions with any but the briefest of answers. It was as though they perceived the answers as self-evident, and not requiring further elucidation or explanation. This was so even for questions which were concerned with complicated topics evoking a great variety of different responses. It was in marked contrast to my previous studies, which had involved interviews with battered women and with mothers of handicapped children, and which had been characterised by long and thoughtful replies by respondents. By contrast it seemed as though family finance was a topic which couples rarely discussed, and which was not the subject of gossip with friends, so the people we interviewed had few ready-made answers and small repertoires of anecdotes, opinions, explanations and justifications. The absence of a 'normative vocabulary' related to the allocation of money within the household has been noted by other researchers (see, for example, Brannen and Wilson, 1987, p. 10 and Wilson, 1987, p. 84). The difficulty many respondents had in explaining, for example, why they organised their money in the way they did, made me feel that I should have used a more ethnographic and explora-tory approach, at least at this stage in public awareness of the topic.

The study also raised in an acute form the question of what happened after each interview ended. This is an aspect of research which is rarely discussed in the methodological literature. It is recognised that being interviewed can be a profound experience: whether the respondent experiences pain or pleasure, catharsis or apathy depends on the topic, on the interviewer and on the indivi-dual concerned. In this case, the respondents were being asked about a topic which is for some people both very private and very emotive, and they were being asked about it in circumstances which could give rise to considerable tension. Cultural norms about the unifying effect of marriage are implicitly challenged by separate interviews. Either or both of the partners may have financial secrets, or the couple may have financial problems which give rise to guilt, anxiety or mutual antagonism. During the interview each respondent is likely to have felt a variety of different emotions. Being aware that his or her partner was being asked similar questions must inevitably have led to curiosity and apprehension about what was going on in the next door room. The departure of the interviewers is likely to have been the signal, at least, for the comparing of notes about what had been asked and what divulged; in some instances, when the discrepancies between the answers of wife and husband had been particularly great, we went away feeling very anxious about our responsibility for post-interview marital rows.

On the other hand, it has to be recognised that for some couples money simply was not an important issue. The interviews varied greatly. Some respondents began by being reluctant and remained apprehensive throughout the evening; others were happy to be interviewed and answered the questions with interest and eagerness;

others seemed puzzled that the topic should be of any significance and responded to questions laconically and without enthusiasm. For some couples it seemed to be a matter of principle to treat money and financial issues as essentially unimportant. The fact that the information which we collected varied greatly in its significance to the people from whom we collected it must affect the way the results are interpreted. This problem affects all empirical research to a certain extent, but its impact will be greatest when the seriousness with which respondents approach the topic varies so much.

Husband and wife were interviewed first together and then separately, and interviews were completed with 102 couples. The small numbers and the low response rate means that it would be rash to claim that the respondents were representative of a wider population of families. However, in many respects the study couples had characteristics which one would have hoped to see in a representative sample. At the time 48 per cent of married women with children in Britain were in employment, while the proportion in the study sample was 50 per cent. In Britain as a whole 88 per cent of married men with children were employed, while the proportion among the men who took part in the study was exactly the same (Office of Population Censusus and Surveys, 1985). Nearly three quarters of the couples owned their own homes, a proportion very similar to the figure for married couples in England as a whole (Department of the Environment, 1981). In terms of social class and of the ownership of consumer durables the study couples were again similar to the total population of households with children in Britain at the time. The main difference was that the study sample contained smaller proportions of households from the extremes of the social spectrum, so that the very rich and the very poor were both under-represented. The characteristics of the study couples are described in greater detail in appendix 1.

In general, then, the couples who took part in the study were reasonably similar to the larger population of married couples with dependent children in Britain. There is therefore some justification for using the interview data as a basis for developing a better understanding of how married couples allocate their money and what particular patterns of allocation mean for individual men and women.

5

Patterns of money management

Of the 102 couples half the women and most of the men were in paid employment at the time of the interview. All the women were in receipt of child benefit, since all had at least one child under 16, and all the men who were not in employment received either unemployment benefit, invalidity benefit or supplementary benefit (now income support). Thus every individual who took part in the study had some form of income, whether as wages, salary or social security benefit.

About half the sample also had some savings, held either jointly or individually. In all 54 couples had joint savings but these were usually quite modest: only nine couples had joint savings of over £1000. Wives were more likely than husbands to have individual savings but these typically took the form of small, personal nest eggs; 50 wives, but only 29 husbands, had savings of under £1000. When men did have individual savings these tended to be more substantial and ten husbands, as opposed to only four wives, had savings of over £1000 held in their own name. Unfortunately there were no really wealthy people in the sample.

As Table 5.1 shows, the conditions of their paid employment were rather different for men and women. In general, men worked longer hours, with 70 per cent doing paid work for 40 or more hours each week, compared with 16 per cent of the women; this, of course, reflected the women's responsibility for child care, since all these couples had at least one child under 16. Compared with the men, the women were likely to be paid weekly rather than monthly, and they were much more likely to be paid in cash: half of the women, but three-quarters of the men, received their earnings as a cheque or direct debit to a bank account.

Fringe benefits from employment were much more generous for men than for women. Table 5.1 shows that few women were contributing to private pension schemes or to private health insurance and few were members of unions. The low rate of involvement in pension and health schemes is partly a consequence of the ineligibility of part-time employees (Martin and Roberts, 1984, p. 48). By contrast, more than half of the men were contributing to private pension schemes, a fifth had private health insurance and two-fifths were members of unions. When we come to consider the savings held, individually or jointly, by the couples who took part in the study, the wealth held in the form of entitlement to pensions must be seen as part of the total. Fringe benefits accruing from employment are another sort of wealth. Again male employees were more likely to receive these benefits than were female employees, whether they took the form of help with the costs of travel, the supply of tools or of sports facilities, or the giving of a Christmas bonus. The only respect in which women's employment approached

Table 5.1 *Conditions of employment of study couples*

		Women (N = 51) %	Men (N = 90) %
Hours worked weekly:	Less than 29	69	—
	30–39	14	30
	40–49	12	37
	50 +	4	33
Wages/salary paid:	weekly	68	53
	monthly	23	42
	other	9	4
Paid in the form of:	cash	48	25
	cheque/direct debit	52	75
Deductions from pay for:	private pension	8	59
	health insurance	4	19
	union dues	13	39
Fringe benefits as:	help with travel	15	52
	goods	33	42
	tools supplied	8	33
	sporting facilities	6	34
	Christmas bonus	27	47

that of men was in the possibility of getting goods from the place of work, such as free beer from the brewery or apples from the fruit farm.

In the amounts which they earned there were substantial differences between husbands and wives. The take home pay of the women in the sample varied from £2 to £81 per week, while that of the men varied from £29 to £300 per week. Other sources of income included, for wives, child benefit, and for both partners earnings from second jobs, interest on savings, gifts from relatives, loans and gambling wins. The total net income per week of each partner is given in Table 5.2. However, there are many problems with this table. First, it is impossible to present total income accurately in terms of pounds per week. The income of self-employed people can rarely be calculated in this way; interest on savings comes twice yearly and gifts and gambling wins are by nature spasmodic. Secondly, there is the problem of whether respondents declared their true income. Undoubtedly all will not have told the whole truth. However, the questionnaires were designed to minimise the possibility of money being 'forgotten', questions about income and savings were asked in different ways at different points in the interviews and spouses were questioned about each other's income. All this provided some checks on the tables given, but it must be remembered that, especially among the higher earners, there is likely to be a degree of underestimation.

Tables 5.1 and 5.2 portray very clearly the inequality between men

Table 5.2   *Total net income of study couples*

		Women %	Men %
Income per week:	up to £19	34	—
	£19–£57	49	6
	£58–£95	15	23
	£96–£134	2	32
	£135–£172	—	23
	£173 +	—	17
	Total per cent	100	100
	Total number	102	102

and women in the labour market: at the time of the interviews the mean wages of full time female workers were 66 per cent of those of male workers (Central Statistical Office, 1986). However, this inequality is exacerbated by responsibility for young children, which tends to limit the number of hours women can work outside the home, to force them into less well paid jobs and in some cases to prevent them from taking employment at all. Since all the couples who took part in the study had at least one child under 16 they were at the stage in the life cycle when gender inequalities are at their greatest. The disparity in income between men and women means that in the great majority of marriages there has to be some sharing of resources if the women and children are not to live at a lower standard of living than the men. Every couple has to devise some arrangement by which this transfer of resources can take place. Though many never consciously decide to organise their finances in one way or another, in every case there is a describable system of money management.

Couples manage their money in an infinite variety of different ways, but it is impossible to make sense of the complexities of reality without a degree of systematisation. Various typologies of money management had been developed by previous researchers and these influenced the early stages of the investigation. However, ideal types never correspond exactly to the reality of any one situation, as case studies demonstrate. So the first half of this chapter outlines the original typology and uses case studies as illustrative material. Case studies also make it clear that money management has many different dimensions and that adequate systematisation depends on taking into account more elements than can be encompassed within any one typology. The second half of this chapter explores management and control and the relationship between the two, as a basis for the following chapter, which is concerned with explaining why patterns of allocation differ so greatly.

What criteria are appropriate for distinguishing one pattern of money management from another? In the interviews this question was approached in a number of different ways. In the joint interviews couples were asked which partner was responsible for spending on a range of items which most couples have to purchase: this produced a relatively objective, but limited, way of looking at what happened to money within each household. They were also asked two open-ended questions: 'In very general terms, how do you organise the money that comes into the house?' 'Would you say that in general you have separate spheres of responsibility or does it not matter which one of you pays for what?'

Moving from the joint to the separate interviews meant a move from a jointly constructed view of reality to two, more individual views. Sometimes the three versions were almost identical; at other times husband or wife, or both, produced accounts which were radically at odds with the impression they had given in the joint interview. In the separate interviews there were a number of different questions concerned with the control of money: 'So who would you say really controls the money which comes into this household?', 'Do you feel you have to justify to your husband/wife spending money on some of the things you buy?'. Another very revealing set of questions was concerned with why the couple organised their money as they did: 'Why did you decide to arrange your finances in the way you have described?', 'What are the major disadvantages for you?'. The answers to these questions were used to develop an understanding of money transfers within households, that is to say, to explore what happened to money between the point at which it was earned and that at which it was spent.

Four systems of money management

My first attempt to construct a typology of allocative systems built on previous classifications and distinguished four different ways of organising money (Pahl, 1980, 1983, 1984). There were two main criteria for identifying systems of allocation of money. These were, first, the extent to which each partner had access to the main source of money coming into the household, usually the husband's wage or social security payment, and secondly, the extent to which he or she had responsibility for managing household expenditure. In reality, the four different allocative systems shaded into each other, as will become clear from the case studies and from further analysis.

The first of the four systems is *wife management* or the *whole wage system*. Here one partner, in Britain usually the wife, is responsible for managing all the finances of the household and is also responsible for all expenditure, except for the personal spending money of the other partner. There are several different versions of wife management. Probably the most common form in Britain is the system in which the husband hands his pay packet to his wife, either taking out his personal spending money before he does so, or receiving it back from her. If the wife is also earning she will add her wages to the money given to her by her husband, and will be responsible for all family expenditure. There is a second variation of the whole wage system in which the husband, though he may have handed all his earnings to his wife and expects her to be responsible for making ends meet, yet sees himself as having the right to take money back from her. As we shall see, this can cause great problems in marriages where money is short.

Mr and Mrs Jones were typical of many couples who managed their money in this way. They were both unemployed. He had lost his job as a miner and had so far failed to find other employment, while she gave up factory work when the first of their three children was born eight years previously. All their income derived from social security, in the form of unemployment benefit, income support and child benefit and Mrs Jones was responsible for its management. She described how it worked:

> We don't budget. The money comes and we pay what has to be paid that week. I take out the pay-out money – for the milkman and the meters. Then put aside money for food, then cigarettes for me and he has money to go to the pub.

They have no savings. Out of their total income of £90 per week, Mr Jones got between £5 and £10 for his trips to the pub, cigarettes and gambling. He said.

> I give it to her and let her sort the bills out and I get what's left. She's in more than me really. She knows what there is to pay out. I don't know what there is – all the milk bills and that. I wouldn't have a clue, me; I buy all silly things, I do.

When asked why they arranged their finances in this way, she said,

> It just happened. When he became unemployed it seemed sensible that I should sort out the money, seeing as we don't have any. I've always had the money to pay the bills. I'm better at it because I worry. I *know* that the bills are being paid. The other way round they wouldn't be.

When asked what the disadvantages of their system were, he replied

'None really – I'm quite happy'; she said, 'I have the worry all the time, what's to be paid out'.

The second of the four systems is the *allowance system*. Married couples who adopt this system typically see themselves as having separate spheres of responsibility in financial matters. In the most common form of this system the husband gives his wife a set amount every week or month, to which she usually adds her own earnings if she has any. She is then responsible for paying for specific items of household expenditure, while the rest of the money remains in the control of the husband and he pays for other items. Thus he has access to the main source of income, while she only has access to that part of it which he chooses to give her. The allowance system has many variations, mainly because of the varying patterns of responsibility. At one extreme a wife may only be responsible for expenditure on food; at the other extreme she may be responsible for everything except running the car, and the system of financial management may come close to the whole wage system.

Mr and Mrs Smith had had an allowance system throughout their married life. He was a sales representative; she used to be employed by Marks and Spencers but at the time of the interview she worked at home looking after their two daughters. The couple owned their modern house and had a car supplied by Mr Smith's employers. His income was £418 per month and was paid directly into a bank account in his name. Mr Smith took £30 from the account every week and gave it to his wife as a housekeeping allowance. With this money, and £11 of child benefit, she took care of the day-to-day needs of the household, paying for food, school dinners, papers and Christmas expenses. He was responsible for paying the bills for the mortgage, rates, fuel, telephone and insurance and for hire-purchase payments on the television, the fridge, the washing machine and the kitchen units. The couple had no savings. When asked who really controlled the money in the household Mrs Smith said that she did, and in one sense this was corroborated by the interviewer's comment that 'he didn't really have any money to spend'. However, asked the same question Mr Smith replied 'I do. In the final analysis I have to sign the cheques'. The discrepancy between their answers reflects the fact that she used the word 'control' to mean the management of cash, while he saw control in terms of having power over the household income as a whole.

Mrs Smith did not feel that she had to justify how she spent the housekeeping money: she commented,

> My husband wouldn't do the shopping around and this makes it easier to feel it is mine. I do the hard work of shopping around.

However, she did not feel that she had any right to spend the housekeeping money on herself; she said 'Food comes first, Michael and the kids second, and me behind'. Thus her responsibility for the management of money conferred responsibilities but not privileges. When asked why the couple organised their money as they did her answer combined practicality and ideology:

> He is the only one who always earns a wage. It's a man's responsibility to look after his family: I'm old fashioned but it works.

However, financial dependence was not always easy for her. When asked whether it bothered her not to have any income of her own, she admitted,

> I miss financial independence. I'd like to feel I'm helping. I sometimes feel I'm a burden to him.

For this reason she valued child benefit: 'Its my one bit of thing I can fall back on; my bit of independence'. She was strongly opposed to the suggestion that child benefit should be paid into bank accounts instead of in cash: 'It would go into my husband's account and be swallowed up instead of being for my use'. Their answers to the question 'If you won or inherited £5000 what would you do with the money?' revealed some of the ambivalence this couple felt towards their finances. She answered 'I would pay off all the debts and buy Michael a new coat and put the rest aside for bills. I don't think he'd like that, he would rather it were spent on me alone'. In the next door room, however, her husband was saying that with £5000 'I'd start a business'. Asked about his wife's response, he said 'She would disapprove – she prefers a bird in the hand rather than two in the bush'.

Mr and Mrs Black regarded the allowance system as the 'natural' way of organising their money. At the time of the interview their income totalled £960 per month and derived from his work as an engineer, from child benefit for their five children and from payments from the Social Service Department for their two foster children. Both partners saw the husband as having overall control of family finances and as being the person who decided how finances should be organised. He was responsible for all the major bills, while she had a monthly allowance of £300 with which she bought food, presents and clothing for herself and the children. He described how their system worked:

> We have a budget account worked out on a previous year's budget. It covers the main bills, car tax, freezer, the children's music and birthdays. Once the money for that has been taken out of my salary we know what we've got left for housekeeping for my wife.

When asked why they had decided to organise their finances in this way, she replied,

> I've never really thought about it. We each took our own role and David decided the best way to do it. He's the provider and I spend my housekeeping. He doesn't do anything without my knowledge. But he thinks I've got enough to do without having to worry about organising the money – it's up to him to provide.

In this last remark Mrs Black provides a neat example of the way in which an ideology about the nature of marriage is reflected in the couple's financial arrangements. This couple also illustrate the way in which allocative systems can overlap. Since they had a joint account they might have been defined as pooling their money. However, Mrs Smith rarely drew money from this account and never did so without her husband's permission, so they were categorised as having an allowance system.

The third of the four systems is the *pooling system* or *shared management*. The classic statement of this system is, 'its not my money; its not his/her money; its our money'. Pooling couples have a joint account or common kitty into which both incomes are paid and from which both draw. Thus both have access to the income entering the household and expenditure responsibilities are more or less shared. Of the 57 couples in the sample who pooled their income only seven described themselves as having separate spheres in spending. Shared management is often represented as expressing a commitment to a partnership model of marriage, though, as we shall see, there are instances where there is very clearly a senior and junior partner.

Mr and Mrs Keith pooled the money he earned as the managing director of a fruit processing business. Mrs Keith had given up her job as a secretary to look after their two small daughters. The couple had a joint account from which both withdrew as necessary. They did not budget and they saw themselves as sharing responsibility for expenditure. Mrs Keith usually paid for food and children's clothes, and she was responsible for the bills for rates and fuel; Mr Keith usually paid when they ate out or went to a pub for a drink; all other items were paid by either one of them.

When the interviewer asked why they decided to run their finances in this way, Mr Keith replied:

> So that we were totally open with each other. I trust her implicitly and she trusts me. I couldn't see that there was any other way. Eventually I was going to be the only one earning; I couldn't just keep it all to myself – that wouldn't be a very fair deal. Basically what we have we share.

Out of earshot of her husband, Mrs Keith replied to the same question:

> When we married we wanted to do everything together. We were both working then and it just carried on. It doesn't bother me not earning because I always have access to money. I don't feel dependent because I work quite hard for it: if it wasn't for the children I would be out at work anyway.

The interviewer commented in the notes she made later:

> As a couple they were totally in agreement about money and it didn't seem to present a great problem. This was a very straightforward and easy interview to do, although some of the questions seemed a bit silly when a couple obviously had no real hang-ups about money and just regarded it as a common pool to be drawn on.

This example illustrates the ideology of equality between husband and wife which often underpins shared management, an ideology which in this case had the effect of making interviews based on the assumption that husband and wife would have different attitudes seem silly. For other couples who pooled their money the ideology of marital equality was not necessarily experienced as such, at least not by the wife, as the next case study shows.

Mr and Mrs Roberts were a couple who had experienced a number of different ways of organising money. They were both in their thirties and lived in an immaculate modern house which they were buying from the local authority on a mortgage. Both had full time jobs, he in a brewery and she in an office, and their earnings went into a joint account in the bank. Both paid bills out of this account and they withdrew a certain amount every week for daily spending; if they ran out, either might return to the bank for more money. However, their current system of money management differed from that of their parents and from that of the early days of their marriage. His father had given his mother a weekly housekeeping allowance, so when they married Mr Roberts carried on the same system. Mrs Roberts at first accepted the allowance system, seeing it as an improvement on her mother's experience. She said:

> There were ten of us. My dad was a real pig. He held on to all the money and drank it. We were very badly off – he never gave her enough.

However, Mrs Roberts became increasingly dissatisfied with the allowance system. She described how she felt:

> When my daughter was small I wasn't working and he used to give me so much a week. I could never manage it at all. I used to have to borrow it off him and he even used to keep a record of what I'd borrowed in a little book. It was awful. But that ended when I had to go to hospital for a month and it gave him a real shock to realise what it cost and he saw how well I did really. Then I just threw the little book away. After that he handed over all his wages.

Mr Roberts described the change in a rather different way, but his account, too, contains statements both about practicalities and about ideologies.

> When we first got married and for a long while afterwards I gave my wife a housekeeping allowance. She had trouble managing sometimes and often kept quiet about it. I came home from work once and she was in tears; she really broke down and said she couldn't manage. She had been keeping it secret and worrying about it. I did some of the buying for a while and I found out how much things cost – I had no idea. So we talked

it over and decided she should spend more on food and both of us should be able to get at all the money.

Mrs Roberts still feels that she is accountable to her husband in a way that he is not to her. Asked 'Do you feel you ever have to justify spending money?', he said 'no'. However, she replied,

> Sometimes. He'll moan when £40 has gone and I have to explain it to him. But I get what I want. If I want a dress I'll get it – I'll get round him slowly afterwards – I'll hide it at the back of the wardrobe till I've won him round!

This example illustrates the extent to which shared management can coexist with deference from one partner to another. In some ways, shared management represents a romantic view of marriage, and just as romance can never really hide the structural inequality of the sexes within marriage, so sharing rarely compensates for the lower earning capacity and the financial dependence of married women.

The fourth and last in the typology of allocative systems is the *independent management system*. The essential characteristic of this system is that both partners have an income and that neither has access to all the household funds. Each partner is responsible for specific items of expenditure, and though these responsibilities may change over time, the principle of separate control over income and separate responsibility for expenditure is maintained.

Mr and Mrs Kent were defined as managing their money independently. He worked as an electrician and she as a nurse; they each had a bank account into which their wages were paid and neither had access to the other's account. Most expenditure was the responsibility of one or the other, with only consumer durables and presents being defined as the responsibility of 'either or both' of them. Mrs Kent's wages were very low and were used for running her car, for her clothes and for personal spending money. She felt that it was important for her to have money which she could use as she chose; she said of her parents,

> Father had the money, mother had none. He was the boss. He totally controlled his wife through his control over money. He was terrible to her – never gave her a penny – also beat her up.

When asked what she would feel about having a joint account, Mrs Kent referred to her mother's experience,

Although we have separate accounts, we're together. It's a nice feeling knowing if you do run out you can go and ask for more. And it's nice if he realises that I'm giving something to the home. This stems from my mother who never had a thing to call her own. No matter how silly it seems, independence is something.

Mr Kent said at first he had found it difficult to accept that he was the breadwinner and he resented the lack of independence involved in sharing his income. Because his wife earned so little he paid most of the household bills and also gave her money for food each week. They could have been classified as having an allowance system, were it not that he had no access to her earnings. When asked what he would feel about having a joint account, Mr Kent returned to the issue of dependence and independence.

I don't think it would be right. A wife should remain partly independent: everybody should be independent. I don't want anybody to be completely dependent on me and I don't want to be dependent on anybody else.

It emerged from the separate interviews that Mrs Kent had a private savings account in a building society, kept 'for an emergency', of which her husband was unaware.

The clearest examples of independent management are found among young professional couples, where both wife and husband earn substantial salaries and where there are no children. There were, of course, no couples like this in the sample. However, when Katharine Whitehorn, writing in *The Observer*, asked working couples to describe how they managed their money many of those who replied described independent management systems (Whitehorn, 1982).* One woman wrote,

We began with a complete separation of our money. There was a kitty for food and bills were rigorously halved. Household items were bought by one or the other of us so that there would be no problems when we 'split up'; thus the fridge is his and the washing machine mine. This policy worked well until we bought the house a few years ago (which) decided us on opening a joint account for 'house' things. It didn't really seem feasible for him to take the wiring away and me the plumbing when we split up.

* *I am extremely grateful to Katharine Whitehorn for allowing me to quote from the letters she received. I should add that she removed all names and addresses before passing the correspondence over to me.*

We still have our own accounts for everything else and keep our expenditure rigorously separate. This results in ludicrous, time wasting, carping sessions about once a fortnight on the lines of 'You owe me £2 for the cinema', 'Well, I paid for the tube fare', 'But I got your bus fare twice last week *and* I settled the paper bill from my own pocket'; 'I bought fish and chips last Tuesday', 'We included that in our last reckoning', *etc.*, *etc.*

Independent management of money is probably more common among cohabiting couples, but it is not confined to the un-married. Another woman wrote,

My husband and I both draw regular salaries – he is an accountant, I am an editor. We have two separate bank accounts and our joint costs are split equally: bills, food, mortgage (half of the tax allowance he receives from the mortgage interest is deducted from my share), drinks, meals out *etc*. We each keep a record of the amount we have paid for joint expenses over the period of a month, and shortly after pay day we settle the difference. The remainder of our salaries we are free to spend without guilt on our individual hobbies, friends and other personal pleasures.

As long as both partners are fortunate enough to be employed, this seems to me to be the most obvious and practical system of cost sharing. We have never had rows over money and, further, we are able to feel that our commitment to each other is firmly based on mutual friendship and not on material dependence. Hence it puzzles me that most of our friends in similar circumstances regard this arrangement as somehow rather in-decent.

Many of those who replied to Katharine Whitehorn expressed similar astonishment at the ways in which other couples organised their finances. A college lecturer, who pooled her income with that of her husband, wrote,

We cannot understand why couples have such odd financial arrange-ments. It goes against the respect, tolerance and partnership which we regard as part of marriage. My husband and I have a joint account and regard everything as 'ours' except our clothes. There are never any arguments about who pays for what.

There are two ways in which this comment is typical of much discourse about money management. First, many people find it extremely hard to understand why others organise their finances so differently and, secondly, many people explain their own system of money management in highly ideological terms. As we shall see in chapter 6, these two observations are not unrelated. I shall argue that the way in which a couple organises its money reflects deep rooted assumptions about the nature of marriage and about relationships between women and men. Different financial arrangements, reflecting different assumptions, present an implicit challenge, especially if a couple do not recognise the links between money and marriage.

It was interesting to note that out of all those who wrote to Katharine Whitehorn four-fifths were women. This confirms experience in the study, where women were much more willing to be interviewed than men. It seems that this is a topic which many women find interesting and important but which many men see as boring, dangerous or irrelevant. The letters showed that, among this mainly middle class group of people, the majority of couples operated some sort of shared management system, although there were also examples of wife-management, of independent management and of wives who received an allowance from their husbands. Is shared management most common among the population as a whole? What can be said about the prevalence of different systems of money management?

Prevalence of the four allocative systems

Table 5.3 shows that in general there has been considerable agreement about the prevalence of different ways of organising money in Britain in the 1980s. Several studies have found the proportion using each system as follows: shared management – about a half; allowance system – about a quarter; wife management – about a sixth; independent management – about a twelfth (Family Finances Group, 1983; Bird's Eye, 1983). However, we have to remember that in the first three columns of Table 5.3, the results come from couples who knew they were taking part in a study of financial matters and who chose to discuss this very sensitive aspect of marriage with an interviewer. It is likely that these samples were biased towards couples who were reasonably happily married and for whom money was not particularly problematic. The fourth column gives data from families with pre-school age children, who were being interviewed about the organisation of health care, and so may have

Table 5.3 *Prevalence of different systems of money management*

	Pahl (1983) %	Family Group (1983) %	Birds Eye (1983) %	Graham (1985) %	Homer et al. (1985) %
Wife management (whole wage)	14	18	14	17	21
Husband management (whole wage)	—	—	5	8	22
Allowance system	22	24	26	41	49
Shared management	56	54	51	31	5
Independent management	9	4	1	3	4
Other/don't know	—	—	5	—	—
Total per cent	100	100	100	100	100
Total number	102	250	711	64	78

included fewer earning wives and more couples for whom money was a problem area (Graham, 1985).

Very different financial arrangements have been described in studies of unhappy marriages. The fifth column in Table 5.3 gives results from a study of battered women in Cleveland, in north-east England. This study documented marriages in which physical violence and domination were associated with a high degree of financial control on the part of husbands (Homer, Leonard and Taylor, 1985). In 22 per cent of cases the husband both controlled and managed all the money coming into the household and many women were effectively left without any cash at all. The effect of this on women and children has been documented in other studies of battered women (Binney, Harkell and Nixon, 1981; Pahl, 1980). Even when money was transferred to the wife for housekeeping expenses, many violent husbands expected to get cash back for their own personal use, for example, for drinking and gambling. The financial problems associated with these marriages were reflected in considerable material deprivation among the wives and in the fact that 55 per cent reported that they felt 'better off' living on supplementary benefit after the marriage ended (Homer, Leonard and Taylor, 1985). It seems likely that financial arrangements change in marriages which are near breaking point and that earners become less willing to share with non-earners.

Management and control

The typology of allocative systems used so far in this chapter was based on the work of previous researchers, on historical evidence and on personal experience. But how valid is the typology? What is the relationship between money and control? The rest of this chapter is concerned with exploring these issues. However, there are a number of preliminary points which must be made.

First, there is the question of how the study couples were classified in terms of the four systems of money management. Classification was done by the interviewers on the basis of the answers given in the joint interview. The reason for this was that in the individual interviews the questions which a couple were asked depended on the way they organised their money. A complicated system of skips within the questionnaire ensured that as far as possible couples were only asked questions which made sense in terms of their way of organising money. Though many couples, like those described in the case studies, were easy to classify, others were extremely difficult. For example, if a couple had a joint account, but the only cheque book was kept by the husband who gave his wife a weekly housekeeping allowance, should this be classified as shared management or as an allowance system? In reality, the different types were not mutually exclusive, and for many couples it was a case of choosing the type of allocative system which most closely resembled the way in which they organised their money. As so often in the social sciences, classification involved simplification. It is therefore justifiable to be sceptical about the adequacy of the typology.

Secondly, there were the problems which occur when theoretical concepts are put to the test of empirical reality. For example, in planning the study I had made a distinction between 'control' and 'management'. However, the interviews showed that many respondents did not share my definitions of these terms. In the joint interviews each partner was asked 'In very general terms, who would you say manages the money that comes into this house?' In the separate interviews husband and wife were each asked 'Who really controls the money that comes into the household?' In the *joint* interviews only three couples gave different answers, even though each partner was asked for his or her opinion about who 'managed' the money. However, in the *separate* interviews 29 of the 102 couples disagreed about who 'controlled' the money.

Comparisons between the answers relating to management and control produced some unexpected results. For example, among the 14 couples classified as having a wife-management system, all the wives, and all but one of the husbands, said when they were interviewed alone that the wife 'controlled' the money. However, in the joint interviews 12 of these 14 couples agreed that the husband 'managed' the money. What do these results mean? The joint interview seemed to be an occasion for the development of consensus and for the presentation of a united front. This often involved the expression of ideological statements reflecting traditional notions about the nature of marriage and about male control of money. In the case of households where wives controlled the money it may be that the reality of the wife's power in financial affairs had to be concealed, for the sake of the husband's pride, by a public statement about his management role. On the other hand, it may be that the husband's receipt of wages or social security payment really did give him greater power and that couples were using the word 'management' to mean what I have called overall control and the word 'control' to mean what I have called day-to-day management. Whatever the underlying explanation for these results it seemed as if the answers relating to 'control', given in the separate interviews and so away from the joint presentation of marital harmony, were likely to come closer to 'reality'. Accordingly it is upon the answers about 'control' of money that the following discussion centres.

The interview data produced a number of alternative ways by which to classify the control of finances. These included which partner was seen as controlling the money, who was normally responsible for paying the major household bills and whether responsibility for spending was seen as separate or shared. In the next few pages we examine these aspects of financial arrangements in order to see how they relate to the typology of allocative systems and to each other. *Control of money* was defined by the answers given by wives to the question 'Who really controls the money that comes into the household?'. The husband was said to be in control in 36 per cent of cases and the wife in 40 per cent of cases, while control was shared by 24 per cent of couples. *Responsibility for household bills* was derived from a question in the joint interview where the couple were asked who was usually responsible for spending on particular items. The answers concerning spending on rent or mortgage, rates, fuel, house insurance and consumer goods were combined to form a spending score. This score distinguished households where husbands were responsible for all or most of these bills from those where wives were mainly responsible or where bills were paid by either partner or jointly. Paying the major bills was the responsibility of the husband in 41 households and of the wife in 29; in another 32 households bills were shared between the partners or paid out of joint monies and out of a joint account.

How, if at all, did these different measures relate to each other? Did controlling the money mean paying the major bills, or did it mean being able to hand over the work of paying to the other partner? Table 5.4 shows that there was a strong correlation between the control of money and responsibility for bills. Where the husband was responsible for paying major bills, only five out of 41 wives saw themselves as being in control of finances; where wives were responsible for the bills only three out of 29 described their husbands as controlling the money. A similar association existed between responsibility for bills and the husbands' definition of who was in control of the money, though the differences between husband control and wife control were less marked when the husband was describing the pattern: husbands perceived more equality in the marriage than did their wives. We shall return to this interesting finding in chapter 9.

There was also an association between the control of household money and the way in which couples organised their finances. Table 5.5 shows that when wives managed the money they were likely to see themselves also as overall controller of household finances, while in households with shared management or independent management, wives rarely defined themselves as in control of finances. One might have expected that couples defined as sharing management

Table 5.4 *Control of money by responsibility for main bills*

| Wife sees money as controlled by | Main bills paid by | | |
	Husband	Both/either	Wife
Husband	22	12	3
Both equally	14	9	1
Wife	5	11	25
Total number	41	32	29

Table 5.5 *Control of money by system of money management*

Wife sees money as controlled by	System of money management			
	Wife management	Allowance system	Shared management	Independent management
Husband	—	10	22	5
Both equally	—	7	14	3
Wife	14	5	21	1
Total number	14	22	57	9

would have had equal control, so it is interesting to see that only a quarter of these couples shared control and that husband control and wife control were both more common among shared management couples than equal control. Again the pattern was very similar whether we take the wife's or the husband's answer about which partner controlled the money, except that husbands were more likely to see money as jointly controlled than were their wives.

We have seen that paying the major bills was associated with controlling household finances: was it also related to the way in which couples organised their finances? Table 5.6 shows that there was an association between the system of money management and responsibility for spending. When wives managed the money they were likely to be responsible for the main bills, while in households where the husband gave his wife an allowance or where the partners managed their money independently, the major bills were likely to be paid by the husband. In many ways this correlation was predictable, since one of the criteria for defining allocative systems was the

Table 5.6 *Responsibility for main bills by system of money management*

Major bills paid by	System of money management			
	Wife management	Allowance system	Shared management	Independent management
Husband	—	14	20	7
Both/either	1	5	23	2
Wife	13	3	14	—
Total number	14	22	57	9

pattern of expenditure within the household. However, the table provides reassuring confirmation that this criteria was taken into account when the interviewers classified the couples according to the typology of allocative systems. Couples who managed their money jointly were likely to be jointly responsible for bills, though this may reflect the prevalence of joint accounts in these households. However, there were many pooling households where either husband or wife were responsible for bills; taken together, Tables 5.5 and 5.6 raised questions about the accessibility of 'pooled' money when one or the other partner was seen as controlling resources.

Pooling: ideology and reality

At the end of the joint interview couples were classified by the interviewers according to the typology of systems of money management outlined earlier in this chapter. Of the 102 couples, 57 were classified as pooling their money; the great majority of these claimed that they shared responsibility for financial management. It was not necessary for both partners to be earning in order for them to be defined as pooling their money: what mattered was that each should have equal access to the couple's financial resources. Many spoke eloquently about the importance of equality in marital finances and presented the sharing of money as an expression of deeply-held values. Thus a miner, whose wife worked in a factory, said,

> Marriage is a joint partnership. I'm not entitled to say 'You're not having it': it's there for both of us. It's no use one of us being domineering because nothing would work like that. I wouldn't want to keep our incomes separate – I earn more than my wife and I don't think it would be fair. It equalises incomes putting them into a joint account.

Many couples described their financial arrangements in normative terms. A carpenter said 'A pool system is how it should be: a his/her system would lead to problems such as arguments'. An art director said, 'We're adult people and that's the way it should be done'.

Yet as we have seen, there were many ambiguities about the realities of shared management. The interviewers sometimes remarked on the disparities between the claims made by the couple in the joint interview and the practical realities described in the separate interviews. In the notes made after one such interview they noted,

> There was some confusion about which type of system to categorise this couple in. The joint interview gave the impression that they were a pooling couple, but in the individual interview it became apparent that the wife never really handled money, although she did legally have access because of the joint account. The husband (the only earner) always went to the bank and wrote the cheques. The wife saw child benefit as her only really independent source of income; she stated that she felt a difference between this money, which she had autonomy over, and her husband's salary, which she had to ask to use.

This interviewer's comment raises many problematic issues. It mentions various different aspects of money management and makes it clear that sharing could be more or less complete depending, for example, on whether there was a joint account, which partner checked the statement for the account, who paid the major bills for the household, whether spending had to be justified to the other spouse, whether one partner gave the impression of greater authority in money matters, and so on.

The disparities between the joint and the separate interviews, between ideology and reality, between the protestations of conjugal equality and the practicalities of married life, made it seem as if pooling was yet another 'black box'. In opening up the black box two questions were important. First, among couples claiming to pool their money, were the different parts of money management shared out so as to preserve a balance of power and responsibility, or was there a tendency for one partner or the other to accumulate functions so that power was concentrated? Secondly, among couples claiming to pool their money, were the different parts of money management undertaken by one partner or the other according to choice and personality, or did the division of responsibilities reflect the different structural positions of husband/wife? The second question must await chapter 6, which is concerned with explaining patterns of money management; in the rest of this chapter we investigate shared management and its relationship to overall control.

Table 5.7 compares shared management couples with the rest of the sample. There are three interesting points about this table. First, in terms of both income and capital, pooling couples did have a greater degree of jointness in the way they organised their finances. The majority had a joint bank account and many had a joint building society account and joint savings; those lacking these characteristics typically did so because of poverty rather than for any ideological reason. Secondly, even though the first three items in the table might be considered matters of fact rather than opinion, some husbands still gave different answers from their wives. It is hard to say why this happened. Was it a consequence of error, of deliberate concealment, or simply of different interpretation of the question? At all events the table casts doubts on the validity of data about marriage which is collected from just one partner.

Thirdly, Table 5.7 introduces the important issue of spouses having to account to each other for what they have spent and suggests that wives are rather more likely than husbands to feel they have to justify spending to their partners. This difference holds throughout the sample but it is particularly marked among couples defined as managing their money jointly. It appears that shared management is associated with increased accountability for wives but not for husbands.

What did shared management mean in practice? In theory it might involve all income being kept in a joint bank account or common purse to which both partners had access, both being involved in all decisions concerning money and in checking accounts, and neither having overall control or authority. Was this the pattern, or did couples adopt some division of labour which diminished the togetherness with which they handled their finances? The ways in which couples used their joint bank accounts provided an opportunity to explore this question.

In the sample as a whole there were 51 couples who were defined as sharing management who had a joint account and who checked

Table 5.7   *'Pooling' couples compared with other couples in the sample: wives' answers (husbands' answers in brackets)*

Number who had	'Pooling' couples N = 57	Other couples N = 45
A joint bank account	50 (51)	16 (17)
Joint savings	38 (38)	16 (16)
A joint building society account	30 (27)	12 (13)
To justify spending to their partner	22 (15)	10 (9)

the statement when it came. Checking was the responsibility of the wife in 24 couples, of the husband in 18 cases and of them both in nine cases. Thus already we can see that there was a division of labour. But was this division part of a random sharing out of financial tasks or was it part of a more general pattern in which one partner or the other had greater financial power? Certainly one couple made a distinction between checking the bank statement on the one hand and having responsibility for bills and overall control on the other hand. When asked who really controlled the money, their replies were as follows:

Husband: I do – I put it all out.
Wife: He does – I check the statement but he controls the money. He decides what's to be spent on what.

However, this couple was a-typical. For the majority checking the bank statement was associated with controlling the money as Table 5.8 shows.

If shared management had been associated with equal responsibility for checking the bank statement and equality in control over money all the responses would have fallen into the central category of the central column of Table 5.8; in fact, only six couples out of 51 did so. All the wives and the majority of the husbands who checked the bank statement were also seen as controlling household finances.

Other dimensions of financial power raise the same issues. We have seen that in the sample as a whole there was an association between paying the main bills, checking the bank account, having overall control of family finances and being authoritative about money: the partner with one of these characteristics tended to have the others too. Was the same true of shared management couples, or did the ideology of pooling override the typical pattern? Tables 5.8 and 5.9 together provide the answer. They show a pattern very similar to that found for the sample as a whole. The partner who controlled the money tended to take responsibility for the main bills and for checking accounts. In other words, among pooling couples, as among the rest of the sample, there was a division of labour, so that financial power lay in the hands of one partner or the other: few shared equally in money management. Couples who managed their money jointly claimed a greater degree of sharing and expressed more jointness in their banking arrangements, but in their practice

Table 5.8 *Checking of bank statement by control of money among 'pooling' couples*

Bank statement checked by	Wife sees money as controlled by		
	Husband	Both equally	Wife
Husband	15	3	—
Both	3	6	—
Wife	2	3	19
Total number	20	12	19

they, like the rest of the sample, revealed a fundamental distinction between wife control and husband control in financial affairs.

Four patterns of control

It seemed important to try to clarify the issue of control, and especially its relationship to management. The existence of joint and separate bank accounts offered a relatively objective way in which to assess the jointness or otherwise of a couple's financial arrangements. Having a joint bank account suggested some degree of sharing, so couples with a joint account were divided from those without. Next the couples were sorted according to the wife's answer to the question 'Who really controls the money that comes into this house?'. The possible answers to the question were 'wife', 'husband', 'both'. However, 'husband' and 'both' were combined. This was

Table 5.9 *Control of money by responsibility for main bills among 'pooling' couples*

Wife sees money as controlled by	Main bills paid by		
	Husband	Both/either	Wife
Husband	11	9	2
Both equally	7	6	1
Wife	2	8	11
Total number	20	23	14

because couples where 'both' were said to control the money had financial arrangements which in many respects resembled those of couples where the husband controlled the money more closely than those where the wife was in control.

Some might question the use of the wife's answer to the question on control, preferring to use either the husband's answer, or a combination of the answers from both partners. The analyses described here and in the following chapters were carried out using all three different answers. Thus, for example 'wife-controlled pooling' characterised by the existence of a joint account and by the identification of the wife as controlling the money, was defined, first, by using the wives' answers, second by husbands' answers and thirdly, by both their answers when they were in agreement. The results showed that the associations which existed between financial control and other aspects of the couples' lives were very similar whichever set of answers was used, though levels of significance varied. The general tendency was for analyses using wives' answers to be more statistically significant; that is, more variation existed which was unlikely to have occurred by chance.

Sorting the couples in this way produced four categories. The first category contained couples where there was a joint bank account and where the wife described herself as controlling the money. There were 27 of these and they were described as 'wife-controlled pooling'; they could have been described as 'wife control/shared management' but this seemed rather a cumberous phrase. Among these couples it was usually the wife who paid the bills for rates, fuel, telephone and insurance. In the majority of cases, neither partner had a separate bank account and all finances were handled from the joint account.

The second category contained couples where there was a joint bank account, but where the wife considered either that the husband controlled the finances or that they were jointly controlled. There were 39 couples in this category, which was designated 'husband-controlled pooling'; again, it could have been described as husband control/shared management. Among this group husbands were typically responsible for the bills for rates, fuel, telephone and insurance and for paying the rent or mortgage.

Lack of a joint account implied one of two things. Either the couple were paid in cash and were too poor ever to need a bank, or one or both partners rejected the idea of a joint account. The third

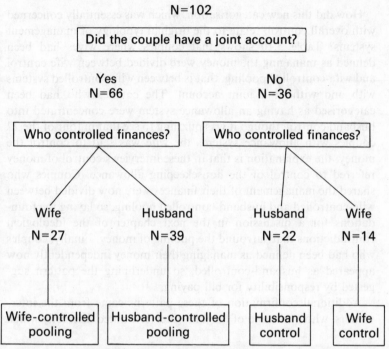

Figure 5.1 *Control of finances*

Note: The wife's definition of who controlled finances was used for the reasons given on page 88. When she said that they 'both' controlled the money this was included in 'husband control', since these couples had financial arrangements which resembled those of couples where the husband controlled the money more closely than those where the wife was in control.

category contained couples where there was no joint account and where the wife considered that control was in the husband's hands or was joint. There were 22 couples in this category, which was described as 'husband-controlled'. Typically the husband had his own personal bank account and he was responsible for all the main bills.

Finally, there was a small group where there was no joint bank account and the wife considered that she controlled the finances. This category contained 14 couples and was described as 'wife-controlled'. These couples typically had no bank accounts at all and operated in cash, with the wife controlling and managing the finances and taking responsibility for the major bills.

How did this new categorisation, which was essentially concerned with overall control, relate to the original typology of management systems? Table 5.10 shows that couples where wives had been defined as managing the money were divided between wife control and wife-controlled pooling, that is between wife-controlled systems with and without a joint account. The couples who had been categorised as having an allowance system were concentrated into husband control, though it was puzzling to see that in four of the 22 couples with allowance systems the wife was said to control the money; the explanation is that in these interviews control of money referred to control of the housekeeping allowance. Couples who shared the management of their finances were now divided between wife-controlled and husband-controlled pooling, so laying the foundations for a discussion in the next chapter of the ideological contradictions that surround the pooling of money. Finally, couples who had been defined as managing their money independently now appeared as husband-controlled, so underlining the pattern suggested by responsibility for bill paying.

Additional confirmation of these patterns came from the interviewers, who at the end of the joint interview noted discreetly which

Table 5.10   *System of money management by control of finances*

System of money management	Control of finances			
	Wife control	Wife controlled pooling	Husband controlled pooling	Husband control
Wife management	7	7	—	—
Allowance system	4	1	4	13
Shared management	2	19	31	5
Independent management	1	—	4	4
Total number	14	27	39	22

Note: There is a difference between the terms 'control of money' used in Tables 5.4, 5.5, 5.8 and 5.9, and 'control of finances' used in this and subsequent Tables. 'Control of money' refers to the wife's answer to the question 'Who really controls the money in this household?'. 'Control of finances' is a typology of different financial arrangements. It distinguishes couples according to, first, whether or not they have a joint account, and secondly, according to which partner is named in answer to the question 'Who really controls the money in this household?' (see Figure 5.1). The aim is to be able to distinguish between the management and control of money by having two typologies, the first being the *system of money management* and the second, the *control of finances*.

partner had been the most authoritative in talking about money. A very significant correlation existed between the husband appearing authoritative in the joint interview and his being described by his wife in her separate interview as controlling the money: conversely wives who appeared authoritative were likely to control the money.

This chapter has been concerned with different ways of classifying financial arrangements. The impossibility of getting a perfect fit in the correlations is very frustrating. This was true whether the couples were being classified according to more objective criteria, such as the existence of a joint bank account and the responsibility for particular bills, or according to subjective criteria based on the opinions of the respondents or the interviewers. One can only remember that the infinite variety of social and economic life means that there will always be exceptions to every generalisation, so that we have to be content with identifying tendencies rather than searching for perfectly correlated certainties.

However, the conclusion of this chapter is relatively clear. Where a wife controls finances she will usually also be responsible for money management; where a husband controls finances he will usually delegate parts of money management to his wife. Thus where a wife controls finances she will usually be responsible for paying the main bills and for making sure that ends meet, as well as for buying food and day-to-day necessities. Where a husband controls finances he will typically delegate to his wife the responsibility for housekeeping expenses, sometimes giving her a housekeeping allowance for this purpose. Marriages where the wife controls the money and the husband manages it are rare. Finally, there is a small number of marriages where the husband both controls and manages the money; Wilson described male control of expenditure as a deviant pattern which has serious consequences for women and children (Wilson, 1987, p. 215). The evidence suggests that when a husband both controls and manages the money there is likely to be extreme inequality between husband and wife and deprivation on the part of the wife and children.

6

Explaining patterns of money management

This chapter is concerned with explaining why married couples differ in the way they organise their finances. Why are the financial affairs of some couples managed by wives and some by husbands, while others claim to manage everything jointly? Why is overall control sometimes in the hands of husbands and sometimes of wives? Do ways of organising finances differ from one part of the country to another and from one time to another? In answering these questions we shall draw on evidence both from this study and from other studies carried out in Britain and elsewhere over the past 30 years. The discussion is bound to be complex, given the nature of the topic, so in the interests of simplicity, the explanations will be grouped under four headings: practical explanations, psychological explanations, socio-economic explanations and ideological explanations. However, as we shall see, explaining patterns of money management is not a simple matter.

Practical explanations are those which attribute causes to such things as the opening hours of banks, or the form in which wages are paid. A wife, it might be suggested, manages the money because she is able to go to the bank when it is open, because she knows what the children need, or because she is responsible for food and therefore for shopping. On the other hand, it might be suggested that a husband manages the money because the bank is near his place of work, because his wages come as a cheque instead of in cash, or because the rules of the tax system decree that a self-employed person must have a bank account in his own name and not in joint names. Certainly some of the people who took part in the study explained their arrangements in these rather practical terms.

A second possibility is that financial arrangements reflect differences in personality and temperament. Some people are careful, level-headed financial managers, while others let money flow through their fingers like water. Some enjoy money, others hate it, while some are resolutely indifferent to everything financial. Again, when asked 'Why did you decide to arrange your finances in the way you have described?' many couples answered in psychological terms.

Thirdly, financial arrangements may be related to differences in the social and economic structures within which households are located. The level of household income, the employment pattern of husband and wife, their life cycle stage, their responsibility for children or elderly relatives, may all be relevant. Are financial arrangements different at higher as opposed to lower income levels? Do patterns of management and control alter when a wife begins to earn a substantial proportion of the household income? Socioeconomic explanations were less often advanced by the couples who took part in the study, but the results of the research showed that they were very relevant.

Finally, financial arrangements reflect ideological and cultural influences. These too can take many different forms. Belief in the 'naturalness' of inequality within marriage is as ideological as a commitment to equality between wife and husband. Particular geographical areas, occupations or religious groups have their own cultures which may be expressed in the financial arrangements of couples who live in those areas or belong to those groups. The privacy which in Britain surrounds money matters is itself the product of a particular ideology and serves to conceal ideological and structural conflicts behind a screen of taken-for-granted secrecy. As the study progressed ideology became a central issue.

One problem is that practical, psychological, socio-economic and ideological explanations are interwoven. For example, the fact that mothers tend to know better than fathers about the needs of children and that women shop for food more often than men, reflects ideologies about responsibility for child care and domestic labour, as well as economic inequalities between the sexes. The opening hours of banks, and their location in business rather than residential areas, reflect ideological assumptions about who will be using banks and economic calculations about which customers will produce the largest profits. Psychological attitudes to money management may reflect cultural and economic influences, so that a financially deprived childhood might engender a concern with financial security and a drive to control money, while affluence may be associated with indifference to financial affairs. Even taxation policy is essentially ideological, as we shall see in chapter 8.

In setting out to explain patterns of money management I encountered a dilemma. On the one hand, I regarded it as important to accept the validity of the answers given by respondents; on the other hand, as analysis progressed, it became clear that the given answers did not present the whole story. In other words, people are not always aware of the social processes of which they form a part. So the answers which interviewers received to their questions represented data in two rather different senses. First, the answers provided information to be taken at face value, and secondly, what was said and not said in an answer, and the ways in which it was said, provided insights into the subjective world of the person being interviewed. The researcher faces formidable problems in trying to achieve a sensitive synthesis of such different sorts of data, while continuing to respect the expressed opinions of the respondents.

Table 6.1 sets out the reasons which wives and husbands gave when asked 'Why did you decide to arrange your finances in the way you have described?' This was an open-ended question and the answers were coded into categories which coincided roughly with the headings used in this chapter. The table shows that reasons categorised as 'ideological' were given more frequently than any other, particularly by men, over half of whom claimed that their system of money management had been chosen because it seemed 'natural', 'right', or 'the fairest way to do things'. Various 'practical' aspects of money management, such as the form of payment of wages and salaries or access to the bank were also mentioned frequently, though women were more likely than men to put forward these sorts of explanations. The same was true of reasons defined as 'psychological': 33 women, but only 24 men, said that their system reflected the fact that one partner or the other had particular skills in money management. Wives were more likely than husbands to be identified as having such skills, and this was especially true in poorer households.

In the conclusion to this chapter we will assess the relative importance of practical, psychological, socio-economic and ideological explanations. First, however, we examine each in turn, drawing

Table 6.1   *Reasons given by wives and husbands for their system of money management*

		Number mentioning each reason	
		Wives	Husbands
	'Ideological' reasons		
1	System seemed natural/right/fair	41	53
	'Practical' reasons		
2	Seemed more efficient/'it just works for us'	27	22
3	Response to way in which wages/salaries paid	22	19
4	More convenient/one partner able to get to bank	19	15
	'Psychological' reasons		
5	Wife 'better manager' so she manages money	23	15
6	Husband 'better manager' so he manages money	10	9
	'Generational' reasons		
7	Tried to avoid parents' mistakes	5	2
8	Money management similar to parents' system	4	1

Note: Numbers add up to more than 102 because some individuals gave more than one reason.

on both quantitative and qualitative data, and on the results of other research.

Practical explanations

More than half the couples mentioned practical aspects of finances when asked why they organised their money in the way they did (see Table 6.1). However, when couples explained their pattern of money management in terms of practicalities, psychological and ideological statements often appeared as part of the account. Mr and Mrs Harris provided one example of this. Mr Harris used to be a long distance lorry driver but now works as a maintenance engineer; Mrs Harris gave up her job as a dental nurse to look after their three children. His income is paid directly into a joint account to which both have access. When asked why they organised their money as they did, she replied,

Probably because he was away long distance. It was a matter of me doing it – he wasn't there.

Asked the same question, Mr Harris' reply included references to a reaction against his parents and the nature of his own personality, as well as mentioning the practical problems of being a long distance lorry driver:

> One of the things was the way my parents did it. I thought it was a bit unfair giving an amount each week when I didn't know how it had to be spent. Why should a husband decide what a wife has for housekeeping when she knows the prices? Partly also being a long distance lorry driver and getting home late Saturday it was too late to get any shopping. I like to earn money but it doesn't mean much to me. In the pocket I like to spend it – left to my own devices I'd always be running into debt I expect.

The practicalities of life in the forces had shaped the way in which Mr and Mrs Evans organised their money. When they married he was a sergeant and was paid in cash. At that time he did not have a bank account because the NAAFI would only accept cheques from officers. Any spare money was kept in Mrs Evans' own account. Now in civilian life, both their salaries go into a joint account. When asked why they organised their money as they did, she explained,

> My husband used to be in the forces abroad. We always had to have access for both of us because of when he was away. There's been times when I've paid everything.

He also referred back to his years in the army.

> When we married I was a sergeant. You couldn't have a bank account. I would give her whatever currency we were using and keep some for myself. Marriage is a partnership. Basically we've got no secrets from each other. So we've got no financial secrets.

However, it was a partnership with a junior and a senior partner. When they were asked who controlled the money, both said that he did, and Mr Evans added,

> I do, in as much as I log all the statements, check all the bills. She's the financial executive. I'm too idle to cash a cheque – she does that for me. As I keep the statement in my drawer I have overall control. I'm the financial auditor in case I have to growl at my wife.

He, too, mentioned making a conscious attempt to do things differently from his parents:

> Mother was always earning, so she had a very separate independent income. There was always 'his' money and 'her' money. They had separate bank accounts. That's why things are joint in this household.

These remarks raise many important issues. They provide an illustration of the distinction between management, as an executive function involving paying bills and cashing cheques, and control, exemplified here by checking the bank statement and keeping it in 'my drawer'. They illustrate the ambiguities which surround the idea of marriage as a partnership within which resources are shared, when the partners are not equals. Finally they demonstrate the ways in which straightforwardly pragmatic explanations concerned with practical constraints can be interwoven with comments about personality differences between husband and wife and ideological statements about the nature of marriage.

To what extent are financial arrangements shaped by practicalities, such as the form in which wages are received? In a study carried out in the early 1970s Todd and Jones suggested that the form in which the husband was paid was closely associated with which spouse paid the bills for fuel and rates, rent or mortgage. Where the husband was paid in cash the wife was likely to carry out these duties; where he was not paid in cash he was likely to have responsibility for the main bills (Todd and Jones, 1972, p. 29). Todd and Jones gave no explanation for these differences, but it seems likely that being paid in cash was associated with having a low income, which was in turn associated with the wife controlling finances.

Over two-thirds of the husbands in Todd and Jones' survey were paid in cash, compared with only a quarter in my study. This difference reflects the very rapid change, which took place between the two studies, in employers' arrangements for the payment of wages and salaries, a change paralleled by an increase in the number of people with bank accounts. Anecdotal evidence suggests that some men resisted the change, on the grounds that it would make it easier for wives to find out how much their husbands earned. Despite this rearguard action, payment in cash has now become relatively unusual for men, though it is still common among part time and casual workers: 48 per cent of the employed women in my study were paid in cash, compared with 25 per cent of employed men.

It was interesting to see whether responsibility for bills still varied according to whether wages were received in cash or not. The results showed that this was not a significant factor. When a husband was still paid in cash, major bills were just as likely to be paid by him as by his wife. The only association was between bills being paid by 'either or both' partner and the husband's income being paid into a bank account, typically into a joint bank account. This pattern provided some support for the idea of using the presence of a joint account as a key variable, and dividing those without a joint account between husband-controlled and wife-controlled households.

Striking differences existed, however, between households where the husband was paid weekly and those where he was paid monthly. Just over half the employed men in the sample were paid weekly, and when this was the case the wife was likely to be described as managing the money and to be responsible for the rent or mortgage, the rates and the insurance. When the husband was paid monthly he was likely to manage the money and to be responsible for these items. There was, of course, an association between the size of the income and the frequency with which it was paid: monthly paid employees had larger earnings than those who were paid weekly. As we shall see, the lower the household income, the more likely it was that the woman would manage household finances. However, weekly payment of male wages was even more closely associated with female responsibility for financial management than was low income. As an example, Table 6.2 shows the pattern of payments for house insurance. When a wife was responsible for insurance the husband was almost always paid weekly, whereas when the husband was responsible for this payment he was likely to be paid on a monthly basis.

Many of those who mentioned changing from weekly to monthly payment of wages had an allowance system. It seemed as though one way of coping with the uncertainty involved in moving to monthly budgeting was to retain weekly budgeting for food. When asked why they arranged their finances as they did, a surveyor said,

Because I changed from a weekly salary to a monthly. It seemed easier to pay by cheque than save it out of the bank account. We discussed it and

Table 6.2 *Responsibility for house insurance by whether husband was paid weekly or monthly*

House insurance paid by	Husband paid	
	Weekly	Monthly
Wife	19	4
Either/both	10	13
Husband	15	25
Total number	44	41

Note: Nine couples had no house insurance and they, and households where the husband was unemployed, were excluded from the table.

decided to have the money paid into the bank and do all payments by cheque. I usually draw perhaps £30 per week to cover for the weekend and week.

Q. What are the major advantages?

Ease of payment really. I've only got to deal with one source. And the fact that only I can draw cheques is an advantage because I can keep control.

Q. What are the major disadvantages?

If I'm out at work my wife can't get cash out for herself. She also keeps nagging me about having an account.

The change from weekly to monthly payments was experienced as a problem by some wives, who had to alter the time horizon for their budgeting. One woman said,

When I was first married I would have liked to have had a husband who was paid weekly who handed over cash. Just for the first few months I found it was alarming. I hadn't ever handled anything except my own wages (as a library assistant). I had no idea how my parents handled their money. I found it hard to deal with *monthly* wages.

Q. What are the major advantages of the allowance system for you?

I feel I know where I am with it. I feel I know how much I've got to call on. We've never discussed a joint account – I would rather not have one.

Moving from weekly to monthly payment of wages could have the effect of reducing the spending power of women, as their previous responsibility for paying a range of bills in cash was reduced to paying for food out of the housekeeping allowance.

It is interesting to speculate about the implications of different time horizons in spending. Budgeting on a weekly basis is the product of weekly paid wages, but it is also related to budgeting for food, much of which is bought on a weekly or a daily basis, and to poverty, which tends to be associated with a little-and-often pattern of expenditure. It is significant that in Britain rent is usually paid on a weekly or fortnightly basis, while mortgage re-payments by owner occupiers are typically paid monthly. Fuel bills are usually paid quarterly, except where a standing order converts them into monthly payments or where a meter ensures that payment is made before fuel is used.

Both time and budgeting are gendered, in the sense that weekly budgeting for food tends to be a female responsibility, while budgeting for larger items bought less often tends to be a male responsibility, except in some very poor households. Even in households which essentially operate on a monthly basis, in terms of the receipt of income and the payment of housing costs, housekeeping tends to be calculated as a weekly sum. It is significant that when child benefit was changed from being a weekly-paid benefit to a monthly-paid benefit and mothers currently in receipt of the benefit were given the option of continuing to receive it weekly, 75 per cent chose this option (Pahl, 1985a).

Different time horizons can create their own internal economies. Thus the idea of economising on housekeeping can be separated almost entirely from the idea of economising on housing or on transport. This may partly account for the curious but familiar phenomenon of 'shopping around' to save a few pence on washing powder or vegetables, while at the same time spending lavishly on do-it-yourself materials or on the car. This apparent contradiction exists partly because women are likely to be doing the 'shopping around', while men are likely to be spending on the house and car, and partly because of the different time horizons involved in different parts of the household economy. This example illustrates yet again the fallacy of conceptualising the household as a single economic unit.

Psychological explanations

Analysing the links between money and marriage offers a rich field of investigation for psychologists. However, I did not approach the topic from a psychological perspective and so can only offer some pointers from the data and some suggestions for further research. One problem, which affected the whole study from questionnaire design to data analysis, was that different individuals perceived money so differently. For example, when asked 'If you won or inherited £5000 what would you do with the money?' a domestic cleaner replied,

> I don't know. I've never thought about having that much money to spare. I would hang onto it until I could buy something big with it. I wouldn't just fritter it away.

A managing director answered the question by saying that he would get a new wife! After being told that this answer would not do, he commented on the £5000:

> It's not a lot. It's not very much. I'd just put it in the savings account and spend it if something came up.

Objectively each of these individuals was proposing to take the same course of action, but subjectively each defined the sum involved in a very different way from the other.

As Table 6.1 showed, a third of the wives and a quarter of the husbands explained their financial arrangements by saying that one or the other partner was more skilled at money management. The following is one example of many. In it a school cleaner and a miner, being interviewed at the same time but in different rooms, explain why she manages the money:

> Wife: When we first married Bill wasn't good with money – it burnt a hole in his pocket. So we talked it over and now we have this. (The advantages?) I don't have to worry when the bills come in. It gives me the heebie jeebies if I don't have the money to pay the bills.

> Husband: I think she's the better manager than what I am and she has the time to pick the prices and knows the needs of the house. (The advantages?) I don't have to worry about the money, where it goes and how it goes.

This reply illustrates a common pattern, in which the husband's reluctance to do the work involved in shopping and to bear the burden of budgeting on a low income is explained in terms of the wife's superior skills in money management.

Different attitudes to money could be expressed in quite trivial ways. Each individual was asked how careful they were with money and how careful they considered their partner to be. An agricultural worker said of herself:

> Not very careful. I give too much to the kids – like I let them have an ice cream every day. My mum had 11 of us and I like to feel my two never have to go without like I had to.

Describing her husband, a maintenance engineer, she said,

> He's very careful with money. Lots of things: he won't spend it. He'll always say no to ice creams!

It might be argued that carefulness with money is a personality trait which is relatively independent of economic circumstances; if there is a connection it might be expected to be with the economic circumstances of a person's childhood, as in the quotation given above. However, the results produced interesting connections between current household income and carefulness with money. As Table 6.3 shows, carefulness with money was shaped both by income and by gender. In general, wives were more likely to be seen as careful than husbands, both by themselves and by their partners. This difference was especially marked among low income couples, where more wives than husbands were described as 'very careful' and fewer as 'not very careful' or 'not at all careful'.

In general, both men and women attributed more carefulness to their partner than they claimed for themselves. This was particularly marked among low income husbands, 36 of whom described their wives as very careful compared with only 20 of the wives themselves, and among high income wives, 13 of whom saw their husbands as very careful compared with only three husbands. Low income husbands were the group most likely to be described as 'not careful', both by themselves and by their wives. The extravagant wife, carelessly spending her husband's hard earned money, appears to be a fading myth, at least by contrast with that other mythical figure, the working class husband whose extravagance endangers the living standards of the family: both Table 6.3 and the interview material suggested that he is still alive and still spending money at the expense of his wife and children. As Allan commented:

> The stereotype of housewives being extravagant is ... so far removed from reality that its continued existence can only be understood as a device that helps husbands to maintain their dominant position by undermining the value of their wives' contribution to the management of resources (Allan, 1985, p. 94).

Table 6.3 *Gender, income and carefulness with money*

	Wives' carefulness with money Wives' answers (husbands' answers in brackets)	
Wife described as	*Low income*	*High income*
Very careful	20 (36)	6 (14)
Fairly careful	28 (18)	28 (22)
Not careful	12 (6)	8 (4)
Total number	60	42

	Husbands' carefulness with money Husbands' answers (wives' answers in brackets)	
Husband described as	*Low income*	*High income*
Very careful	14 (19)	3 (13)
Fairly careful	30 (26)	32 (29)
Not careful	16 (15)	6 (5)
Total number	60	42

Note: 'Low income' defined as less than £175 per week.
'High income' defined as £175 per week and over.

Socio-economic explanations

Under this heading we examine the extent to which the management and control of money are associated with such things as the size of the household income, the employment status of members of the household, the relative contribution which husband and wife make to the household budget, their social class, educational attainment, stage in the life cycle, responsibility for dependants, and so on.

Few people mention these sorts of factors when they are asked to give the reasons why they organise their finances as they do. It is hard to see oneself as part of a social category and harder still to recognise the extent to which membership of a given category makes it likely that one will behave in a particular way. For example, if a couple is asked why they had two children, their replies will typically be couched in terms of choice, chance and personal taste; yet a demographer could have predicted that parents living at that time, in that location and in those socio-economic circumstances would have been more likely to have had two children than any other number. This fact does not, of course, detract from the couple's freedom to have no children, or six children, but the reluctance to recognise socio-economic explanations may reflect the uneasiness which people experience when it seems as though their behaviour is determined by forces outside their control.

There is convincing evidence from many studies that in low income households the wife is likely to manage the money (Edwards, 1981; Family Finances Group, 1983; Graham, 1985; Gray, 1979; Land, 1969; Wilson, 1987). Some researchers have presented their results in terms of social class rather than income level, but the conclusion is similar: among working class couples wives are likely to be responsible for family finances (Oakley, 1974; Zweig, 1961). As we saw in chapter 3, there is a long history of female responsibility for finances when money is short.

At higher income levels the pattern is more complicated. The allowance system, in which the husband controls finances while the wife manages a part of the expenditure, is mainly found among better off couples (Edwards, 1981; Graham, 1985; Gray, 1979; Family Finances Group, 1983). However, a variety of other financial arrangements exist at middle and upper income levels. Some researchers have seen shared management as typical of higher income couples (Goldthorpe *et al.*, 1969; Land, 1969; Family Finances Group, 1983). Others have suggested that shared management can be found at all income levels except the very lowest (Graham, 1985; Wilson, 1987). Wilson makes some interesting observations about the ways in which women perceive male ability

to handle money at different income levels, observations confirmed
by the pattern shown in Table 6.3:

> Most low income men were not expected to be good managers even if they
> were good providers. The pervasive idea was that men earned the money
> but that was all they did. Financially they were not to be trusted further.
> Their priorities were wrong and they did not understand about keeping
> out of debt, paying the bills on time and making sure the children came
> first . . .

> At high income levels the view of men was very different. Their ability to
> provide the basics was assumed and most high earning husbands were
> characterised as being good with money and as understanding more
> about it than their wives (Wilson, 1987a, p. 151).

What other factors besides poverty are associated with a woman
managing finances or sharing management with her partner? Several
researchers have found that employed women are more likely than
unemployed women to have a degree of power in financial matters,
especially if their husbands are also employed (Edwards, 1981;
Family Finances Group, 1983; Land, 1969; Wilson, 1987). In her
study of steelworkers in South Wales, Morris raised interesting
questions about the relative significance of socio-economic and
cultural variables. She found that the 'kitty' system, that is shared
management, was more common where both partners were
employed full time, while male control characterised households
where only the husband was employed. However, female control
was most likely to occur where the wife did not have a job or where
both partners were out of work: Morris linked this to the local
culture of South Wales:

> A tradition of sexually segregated social activity, and the allocation of
> domestic responsibility to the woman, seems to be an important factor in
> the pattern of household finance adopted. Although the high incidence of
> female control of income prior to redundancy suggests a local pre-
> disposition towards the adoption of this pattern, shortage of money
> seems likely to accentuate the tendency (Morris, 1984, p. 514). (See also
> Leaver, 1987.)

We will consider the significance of culture and ideology in more
detail in the next section. In the meantime what did my study
contribute to the discussion about the association between socio-
economic characteristics and financial arrangements?

As far as the management of finances is concerned the data from the study confirmed the results of other research. Wife management was more common where the household income was low and the allowance system where household income was relatively high, while shared management was found at all income levels. The source of the income was also relevant, in that when households were dependent on social security benefits, wives were likely to manage the money. When wives earned in their own right the management of money was likely to be shared, while when the husband was the only earner he was more likely to give his wife an allowance, retaining the rest of his earnings to pay the main bills. Where neither partner earned the wife was likely to manage finances. (For detailed tables see Pahl, 1984.) My results were very similar to those found by Edwards in her study of 50 Australian families:

> In lower income families, particularly where the wife did not earn, the wife was more likely to manage the finances. If the wife did earn either she managed the finances herself or she and her husband did so jointly. At higher income levels, if the wife did not have paid employment, the husband was likely either to manage the finances himself or to give his wife a housekeeping allowance. At higher income levels, if the wife did earn, either a shared management system or an independent management system was likely; the latter form of financial management was more likely if the wife made a significant contribution to family income (Edwards, 1981, p. 132).

The independent management system is interesting, not least because it seems to be on the increase. The evidence suggests that it is most commonly found among couples where both partners are in employment and where both earn relatively large amounts: this is the 'yuppie' system (Hertz, 1986; Edwards, 1981; Family Finances Survey, 1983). In the British Social Attitudes Survey there were two categories which are relevant here: these were 'independent – partners keep their own money separate' and 'partial pool – partners pool some of the money and keep the rest separate' (Jowell, Witherspoon and Brook, 1987). Out of a total sample of 1086, 15 per cent said that they organised their finances in one or other of these two ways. However, the proportion rose to 25 per cent among those with a household income of over £18,000. Among couples who were cohabiting but were not married nearly half organised their finances so that all or part of their money was managed independently. It would be interesting to know whether these couples will move towards greater sharing if, and when, they marry, or whether they are part of a generation or culture which values independence in financial matters. The processes by which systems of money management change are complex and mysterious.

Unfortunately, my sample in Kent contained no couples in which both husband and wife earned substantial incomes and few with large capital assets besides their home. Those who were classified as managing their money independently were in many ways similar to those who had an allowance system, except that among the independent management couples part of the wife's allowance came from her own earnings and her husband did not have access to this money. Typically the husband was responsible for paying the main bills and he was defined as controlling the household's finances. Thus my independent management couples were rather different from the young, urban professionals among whom this system is most commonly found.

We have already seen that the *management* of money reflected such things as income level and employment pattern: was the same true of the *control* of finances? In answering this question I shall use the control of finances typology outlined at the end of chapter 5 (see Table 5.10). Tables 6.4 to 6.7 set out some of the socio-economic variables which distinguish between wife control, wife-controlled pooling, husband-controlled pooling and husband control.* *Wife*

Table 6.4 *Control of finances by total household income*

	Household income		
	Low Under £100	Medium £100–174	High £175 and over
Wife control	5	7	2
Wife-controlled pooling	2	16	9
Husband-controlled pooling	2	18	19
Husband control	1	9	12
Total number	10	50	42

* These are just a few of the many statistically significant tables which could have been presented. In order not to overload the text with tables other results are described in the pages which follow. However, detailed figures are available from the author.

Table 6.5 *Control of finances by employment pattern*

	Both employed	Wife only	Husband only	Neither employed
Wife control	5	–	5	4
Wife-controlled pooling	19	–	7	1
Husband-controlled pooling	17	–	19	3
Husband control	9	1	9	3
Total number	50	1	40	11

Table 6.6 *Control of finances by wife's earnings as a proportion of husband's earnings*

	Wife's earnings		
	Over 30% of husband's earnings	Under 30% of husband's earnings	Wife had no earnings
Wife control	6	–	8
Wife-controlled pooling	12	8	7
Husband-controlled pooling	5	14	20
Husband control	5	5	12
Total number	28	27	47

Table 6.7 *Control of finances by social class*

	Both middle class	Husband middle class wife working class	Wife middle class husband working class	Both working class
Wife control	3	2	2	7
Wife-controlled pooling	10	0	10	7
Husband-controlled pooling	18	6	1	14
Husband control	7	2	3	10
Total number	38	10	16	38

control of finances was particularly common in low income, working class households where neither partner had any qualifications. Wife control was associated with the payment of wages in cash and with the absence of any bank accounts. Typically the wife also managed the money, paying for food and for rent, fuel, insurance and so on, while the husband had a set sum for his personal spending money. Thus in many respects wife control was synonymous with wife management.

Husband control was associated with relatively high income levels. Typically these couples had a set amount of housekeeping money, which was given by the husband to the wife as an allowance: she paid for food and daily living expenses, while he paid the main bills. Some of these couples kept their money separate and when this was the case the wife's wages typically went on housekeeping, while the husband was responsible for larger bills. In terms of the management of finances, husband control was associated with the allowance system and, in this sample at least, with the independent management of money. It seemed that husband control was characteristic of the skilled working class couple, where either the husband or both partners were in employment; it may be that this was the system adopted by couples who, as their income grew larger, moved away from the whole wage system managed by the wife but did not acquire the ideology of shared management of money.

This series of tables reveals interesting differences between *wife-controlled pooling* and *husband-controlled pooling*. As Table 6.4 shows, wife-controlled pooling is associated with medium income levels, while husband-controlled pooling is more typical of higher income levels. Table 6.5 shows that wife-controlled pooling is associated with the employment of both partners; when only the husband is in employment he is likely to control the pool. Table 6.6 shows that the more the wife contributes to the household income the more likely it is that she will control household finances; this effect is particularly marked among pooling couples. Where wives' earnings were 30 per cent or more of their husbands' earnings, wives were twice as likely as husbands to control the pool; where wives had no earnings, husbands were three times more likely than wives to control the pool.

Table 6.7 shows control of finances by social class. This table was produced by classifying the current or most recent occupation of each person according to the Registrar General's classification

(Office of Population Censuses and Surveys, 1970). There are, of course, limitations to the validity of the classification system, especially when applied to women (Dale, Gilbert and Arber, 1985). Thus the results must be regarded as tentative. The effect of social class was particularly marked among pooling couples, especially where husband and wife were of different classes. Where the husband was classified as middle class and the wife as working class, the husband always controlled the pool, or joint account. Where the wife was middle class and the husband working class, she controlled the pool in all but one instance. The same pattern occurred for qualifications. If one partner had more qualifications than the other he or she was likely to control finances; where both partners had gained some qualifications after leaving school there was a tendency for the husband to control finances.

One might have expected that control of finances would have been associated with the ages of husband and wife and with their stage in the life cycle. The fact that control of finances correlated both with total household income and with the proportion of that income contributed by the wife suggested that control patterns might have been expected to change as the couple grew older and as their youngest child started school. However, the results showed that this was not the case. It may be that the two variables cancelled each other out. Thus older couples were likely to have higher incomes and higher incomes were associated with husbands controlling finances. On the other hand, when the youngest child was over school age wives were more likely to earn or to earn more and these variables were associated with wives controlling finances.

Table 6.5 contains one anomaly, a couple where the wife was in employment while the husband was out of work. Contrary to what one might have expected, this was a household in which the husband controlled the money. Explaining why this was so introduces the topic of ideology.

Ideology and money in marriage

The term ideology is essentially concerned with the sets of ideas held by individuals and groups, ideas which are rooted in the social and economic circumstances which shape people's lives. An ideology is a coherent system of beliefs and attitudes which serves to make sense of reality and to shape social action. However, since different individuals occupy different positions in society, in terms of material circumstances and access to power, it follows that there will be many different ideologies, which will differ, compete and clash. In any one society at any one time the conflict between ideologies is likely to be concealed by the creation of what Therborn has called a 'discursive order', or dominant ideology:

> The construction of a discursive order in a particular society is the historical outcome of struggles waged by social forces at crucial moments of contradiction and crisis (Therborn, 1980, p. 82).

A discursive order affirms the ideologies of the most powerful groups in society, while devaluing and excluding competing ideologies.

The concept of 'the family' is itself a powerful ideological construct, containing within it assumptions about the nature of relationships between men and women, between children and parents and between other members of the same kin group. Morgan has pointed to the need for more work on the ideologies which surround the notion of 'the family' and especially on,

> the process whereby the link between family, marriage and inequality is obscured or ignored in favour of a model of marriage which emphasises the interpersonal and the relational as against the economic (Morgan, 1985, p. 103).

The idea of 'the family', particularly when it is used synonymously with the conjugal household unit, contains various components which are themselves enduring ideological constructs. These include the concept of the 'family wage', paid to a male 'breadwinner' for the support of himself and his 'dependent' wife and children. The idea of the family wage assumes that one wage will be enough to provide for the needs of all the members of the family, and that the earner will share 'his' wage with them. The idea of the 'breadwinner' and the 'dependent' wife assumes that living standards are maintained entirely by the paid work done outside the household, so making invisible the unpaid work done within the home. The idea that the breadwinner is male is rooted in ideologies about the nature of masculinity and in an acceptance of inequality between men and women.

Studies of couples where the woman rather than the man is the chief earner show the force of the ideologies surrounding the conjugal contract. Female breadwinners somehow have to compensate their husbands for the loss of breadwinner status. Stamp found that breadwinning wives held back from exercising as much power as they might, given their financial contribution, and that they tended to involve their husbands in financial responsibility (Stamp, 1985, p. 22). Hunt described how a husband who chose to swap roles with his wife and be financially supported by her still maintained a strong bargaining position with regard to housework, because of the ideological support for housework being her rather than his responsibility (Hunt, 1978 and 1980). McRae investigated the allocation of money in families where the wife was of higher social class than the husband. She found that the tensions to which this gave rise were often resolved by treating all income as joint funds: thus an ideology of equality, as expressed in financial arrangements, concealed the reality of economic inequality (McRae, 1986, p. 121).

The one couple in my sample where the wife was the breadwinner also dealt with this situation by pooling all their money. Mrs Hedger was a farmworker; Mr Hedger had lost his job as a driver when he was injured in an accident two years earlier and was in receipt of invalidity benefit. Mr Hedger paid the rent and did the daily shopping, the cleaning and weekday cooking while Mrs Hedger was responsible for the other bills and for weekend shopping and cooking. He described what happened before his accident:

> I used to pay the wife housekeeping money and the rest I'd have in my pocket to spend how I liked. Five years ago I used to spend £10 to £15 per night, four or five nights per week. But now I can't – and I can't say I miss it.

Mrs Hedger also described the changes in their financial arrangements:

> He used to give me housekeeping and out of that I had to pay all the bills, rent, food and so on. It didn't work because I never had enough money left. If I was short I could ask for extra, but I tried to manage. When I started work we started putting it together.

In answer to the question 'Who would you say really controls the money that comes into this household?' she said,

He does: he has all the money. I come home and hand him my pay packet – like a fool! Then he hands me back money for food for the weekend and bits for myself. I don't think people believe I hand my pay packet over. Most of the time it's the woman what controls the money, but in our position with him not working its been reversed. With him being at home all day he has to do most of the shopping.

When asked what the advantages of this system were for him, he said,

It's done me good, to be honest – it's taken a lot of responsibility off the wife and drawn me more into the family and the running of the family.

These quotations illustrate the complicated negotiation which occurs when ideology and reality do not coincide. When Mr Hedger was the breadwinner he delegated the work of managing the money to his wife and kept back a substantial sum for his personal use; his wife managed whatever amount he had decided to give her. When their positions changed she did not become a breadwinner in the sense that he had been. He took over the management of most of their income, but control remained with him and this gave him the feeling of being 'drawn more into the family'. It is as though, if he had been neither the breadwinner nor the controller of finances, he would have had no part in the life of the family: that is to say, a subordinate role would not have seemed like any role at all.

Marriage, too, is an ideological construct, and one which draws strength from religious and legal definitions of its proper nature. Thus Adam was said to have been created first, while Eve grew from one of his ribs to be 'an help meet' (Genesis, 2, 18) and St Paul instructed wives to 'submit yourselves unto your own husbands, as unto the Lord' (Ephesians, 5, 22). In the traditional Church of England marriage the wife promised to 'obey and serve' her husband, and though the husband declared that he was endowing his wife with all his worldly goods, until the late nineteenth century in reality marriage marked the point at which all her goods became legally his, as we saw in chapter 2.

Strong religious beliefs dominated the lives of Mr and Mrs Church and were expressed in their financial arrangements. They had a joint account, out of which Mr Church paid all the bills, while Mrs Church used the child benefit for their four children as daily housekeeping money. If she ran short she could draw money from their joint account, but she always let her husband know if she had done this and it was a rare occurrence. When asked why they organised their finances as they did, he said

> Because the biblical principle is that the man is the head of the home and it relieves my wife from these emotional pressures. I would take the strain off those things and pressures which God didn't intend her to carry. (The advantages?) It helps me to be a man and it helps my wife to be a woman.

He saw financial control as shared, but she considered that he controlled finances. Her comments contain within them echoes of conflicting ideologies:

> Because we're Christians we feel that the man should have the responsibility. We feel that the man is the head of the home from the point of view of care and responsibility – and authority when necessary. There's some couples where the woman is more capable. But as a basic principle its a good one, we feel.

When asked 'Have you and your husband always done things this way?' she stopped speaking as a couple, in the first person plural, and began speaking as an individual, but with some hesitation:

> I found it hard initially – thinking that the man's going to do it all, sort of thing. From being single to doing things together. Pete thought it was right for the man to do it, and it worked out alright. But when you've been independent, it seemed a bit hard, sort of thing.

After his interview had ended, and while his wife was still being interviewed in the next room, Mr Church commented that for him women were created from Adam's rib and as such were 'weaker vessels'. There seemed some disparity between this ideology and the reality, in which his wife was feeding six people on £23.40 per week, a feat that was described by her husband as 'marvellous: I don't know how she does it.'

The link between ideology and economic power suggests that there will be ideological differences between people in different material circumstances, between members of different occupational groups and between those living in more or less affluent areas of the country. Evidence on the geographical distribution of different ways of organising money is scanty, and most of it relates to the prevalence of wife management, otherwise described as the whole wage system or 'tipping up' of wages. Several studies have found this system to be most common in the north and north-west of England, and in Wales, and least common in the Midlands and south-east (Gorer, 1971; Family Finances Group, 1983; Todd and Jones, 1972). In a study carried out in the late 1950s the whole wage system was described as 'the Welsh way' by some respondents and as 'the Irish way' by others (Zweig, 1961, p. 35).

Explaining geographical variations is more difficult. Does the fact that the whole wage system is more common in some parts of the country than in others reflect cultural differences between the regions? It has been argued that the whole wage system is found more often in areas with a tradition of female employment outside the home and female power within it, while the allowance system is characteristic of male dominated cultures where there is little female employment (Klein, 1965). It is interesting that a study of a coal mining community in Yorkshire, where few women were in paid work, found that the normal practice was for the husband to give his wife a housekeeping allowance, described as her 'wages' (Dennis *et al.*, 1956). A study carried out at the same date in Lancashire, where there were more opportunities for female employment, found the whole wage system to be the norm (Kerr, 1958). Gray found that the whole wage system was more common among couples where the chief earner was in a traditional occupation, such as farming, fishing or mining, while the allowance system was more common among skilled manual workers or those who ran their own businesses (Gray, 1979). However, as we have seen, the whole wage system is always more common in households with low incomes. It may be that geographical variations, and variations between occupational groups, reflect income levels. It would be valuable to be able to analyse data from a large national sample of households to see whether regional and occupational variations exist independently of household income levels.

A few respondents in the study made explicit links between occupation or employment status and the ways in which they organised their money. For self-employed people it was often necessary for them to have a separate account for the business and this could have the effect of keeping the financial arrangements of husband and wife separate. In a few instances it enabled husbands to maintain themselves at a higher standard of living than other members of the family.

One wife identified farming as a significant influence on their financial arrangements. Mr and Mrs Cox owned a small fruit farm and she had given up her job as a health visitor to look after their two young children. Mr Cox had a business account for the farm, from which he gave his wife £60 per week, for food, petrol and things for the children; he also had a personal current account and a deposit account for larger farm expenditure. Mrs Cox had her own account, set up at the time when she was earning, but it only had a few pounds left in it. When asked what she would feel about having a joint account Mrs Cox said,

> Impossible – because he is self employed. I think he ought to get us a joint account but that's totally against farming religion. I don't like the system, but it's something I've got used to. When I was earning I used to save my money and he used to give me a set allowance to buy food *etc*. It just seemed to carry on from those days.

Mr Cox claimed that he had never thought about having a joint account. When asked why they organised their finances as they did, he found the question puzzling:

> I don't know really: it just seemed easier to have a set amount each week. You get through more money if you keep writing cheques. (The advantages?) I spend less money this way.

At a later stage in the interview Mr Cox commented that most of his friends gave their wives a housekeeping allowance, which suggests that Mrs Cox was correct in identifying this as characteristic of farming families. When asked 'Do you feel you need to justify to your wife/husband spending money on some of the things you buy?', Mr Cox answered 'No', but Mrs Cox said,

> He'll ask – so I feel I have to justify myself. Like the house, he thinks that's his domain. I went out and bought some wallpaper for the kids' room. He didn't like that at all because I did it without his permission and knowledge.

She found it difficult not having any money of her own:

> Because I had it before and I miss it. My housekeeping isn't for me: it is to run the house and the children, not for me. I've always had my own money up to the time I was married. I don't like being dependent. I'm always going on about it and it causes arguments.

These comments illustrate neatly the workings of patriarchy as both ideology and practice. Structural inequality in the labour market was compounded by assumptions about the husband's right to control financial matters and to spend autonomously, a right so taken for granted that he had never really thought about it before the interview. As far as the wife was concerned, the dominant ideology, which she called 'farming religion', assumed that she would defer to the earner, would use his money for the house and children and would accept that because her work was unpaid she had no right to any money for herself. An alternative ideology expresses itself in her resentment and recognition of loss.

Studies of violence in marriage have described a pattern in which an ideology of male dominance is expressed both in physical abuse of the wife and in male control of the couple's money. The Dobashes, in their study of battered women, found that 'the majority of the disputes that preceded the violence focused on the husband's jealousy of his wife, differing expectations regarding the wife's domestic duties and the allocation of money' (Dobash and Dobash, 1980, p. 98). In her study of *Hidden Violence* Evason made important links between wife abuse on the one hand and the nature of marriage on the other hand, with particular emphasis on financial arrangements within marriage (Evason, 1982). Evason interviewed 694 single parents living in Northern Ireland; of these 277 (40 per cent) were divorced or separated women, of whom 155 (56 per cent) had been battered wives. The discovery that more than half of these divorced or separated women had been victims of wife abuse is itself evidence of the prevalence of violence in marriage, and especially among those marriages that end in divorce or separation.

Evason's study focused on the differences between the women who had been battered by their husbands and those who had not. There were no differences between the two groups in terms of education and social class, nor in terms of how long the partners had known each other before marrying, or their ages at marriage. Significant differences appeared between the two groups, however, when attention was focused on the nature of these marriages and on the spouses' expectations and assumptions. The great majority of the wives would have liked a democratic model of marriage with decisions made jointly; by contrast husbands were seen by their wives as much more likely to prefer the traditional, male-dominant model of marriage, in which a husband is 'master in his home'.

Violent husbands were particularly likely to prefer the traditional model, 66 per cent of them favouring male dominance, compared with 34 per cent of the non-violent husbands.

There were further differences between the two groups in the ways in which the couples organised their money. Evason distinguished three models of money management; these were, first, shared management, secondly the allowance system in which the husband gave his wife a regular sum for housekeeping, and a third model in which the husband controlled and managed finances, allocating money to his wife if and when he saw fit to do so. Violent husbands were more likely to adopt the third model and less likely to use shared management than were non-violent husbands. Evason ended by identifying the financial dependence of married women as an important part of the pattern of structured constraints which keeps women within violent marriages (Evason, 1982, p. 76, see also Ayers and Lambertz, 1986).

Financial arrangements in violent marriages were also investigated by Homer, Leonard and Taylor (1984 and 1985). They found that in 67 of the 78 families represented in the study men controlled the finances: some husbands even took the wife's child benefit and one appropriated her maternity allowance to buy clothes for himself. Few of these couples shared management of the money and when there was a whole wage system it was as likely to be managed by the husband as by the wife. However, normal patterns of money management were largely irrelevant in situations where husbands retained the right to withhold money from their wives or to take it back, by force if need be, for their own use. The evidence showed that, for the vast majority of the women interviewed, the husband's exercise of the power of the purse and the force of the fist coincided. The researchers concluded:

Family circumstances are insufficient to explain all the hardship discovered; for, as we have shown, much of the primary poverty of women and children existed regardless of family income level, as a result of the distribution of income within families (Homer, Leonard and Taylor, 1984, p. 15).

Despite the continuation of extreme male dominance in some marriages the evidence suggests that, on the whole, the last 20 years have seen an increase in the prevalence of shared management.

Studies carried out in the 1950s and 1960s tended to find the majority of couples divided between wife management and the allowance system and relatively few couples pooling their money (Zweig, 1961; Gorer, 1971; Land, 1969). Re-analysis of the data collected for Townsend's study of poverty in the United Kingdom showed that the wife managed the whole wage for 13 per cent of married couples, while in 65 per cent of couples the husband gave his wife a fixed amount for housekeeping; only 1 per cent had a joint bank account (Townsend, 1979). Most studies carried out in the 1980s have shown much larger proportions of couples sharing the management of finances (see Table 5.3). To some extent this probably reflects the spread of joint bank accounts, but it seems also to represent a real change in ideology, since all those with bank accounts do not have joint accounts.

The idea of a recent trend towards shared management is confirmed by the data collected in this study. Table 6.8 shows that while the allowance system was predominant among the parents of those who were interviewed, shared management has now taken its place as the most common way of organising money. Some of the changes in Table 6.8 may be due to sampling: the decrease in the whole wage system may have occurred because my sample under-represented the very poor, while the apparent disappearance of the whole wage system managed by the husband probably reflects the fact that husbands who exercised a high degree of control in financial matters usually refused to take part in the study.

There are many possible explanations for the ideological shift represented by the move towards shared management. Some of the

Table 6.8   *Allocative systems of parents of study couples and of the study couples themselves*

	Wives' parents %	Husbands' parents %	Study couples %
Wife management (whole wage)	21	34	14
Husband management (whole wage)	5	3	0
Allowance system	59	45	22
Shared management	14	15	56
Independent management	1	3	9
Total per cent	100	100	100
Total number	78	71	102

shift consists of a move away from the allowance system, which as we have seen is associated with couples where only the husband earns. The employment of married women has increased from 30 per cent in 1961 to 60 per cent in 1981, so that it is now normal for a married woman to have earnings of her own: the effects of this change are likely to be felt even by those women who are not in paid work at any one time. Some of the shift consists of a move away from wife management of the whole wage to shared management. As we have seen, wife management is associated with poverty and, as more couples have attained a degree of modest affluence, husbands have begun to seek a share in money management. Perhaps the most important influence, but one which it is impossible to quantify, is that of the Women's Liberation Movement, in its questioning of male dominance and in its exposure of the ideologies which support and maintain that dominance. It is significant that how married people organise their finances has until recently been largely unacceptable as a topic both for social conversation and for academic study. The growth of a body of research on the topic, much of it carried out by feminists, may be contributing to the creation of a new discursive order.

Conclusion

This chapter has been concerned with explaining patterns of financial management and control, by analysing correlations between financial arrangements and other aspects of the lives of married couples. A correlation is not, of course, the same as a cause, yet the existence of overlapping correlations suggests patterns of causality. The topic is full of complexities. Thus, explanations couched in terms of practicalities or of psychological characteristics were more commonly presented in interviews than other explanations. However, the analysis showed that the socio-economic circumstances of peoples' lives, and the ideologies which shaped their views of the world, often had greater explanatory power.

Different variables become significant in different circumstances. Management and control may be in the same or different hands. Household income is an important variable when income is low: when money is short, so that managing it is a demanding chore rather than a source of power or pleasure, then typically women manage and control finances. At higher income levels the source of that income becomes important. If only the husband is in employment he tends to control the money, and to delegate management of a part of it to his wife. The higher the proportion of household income contributed by the wife the more likely it is that she will control finances. Ideology is a crucial variable, but one whose effect is often difficult to quantify. It can be used as a justification: wives are seen as better at management when money is short, while husbands are defined as financially knowledgeable when there is more money and when the wife's work is unpaid. The ideology of equality within marriage has led in recent years to an increase in shared management. However, among couples who share management of their finances overall control is still related to such characteristics as employment status, qualifications, social class and income contribution.

Figure 6.1 sets out a model which attempts to sum up what has been said in this chapter. The pattern of financial control adopted by a couple is just one element, though a central element, in a complex and dynamic process. In this process it is difficult to differentiate dependent and independent variables because of their inter-relatedness. For example, control of finances is related to expenditure patterns in at least two different ways. If a wife is defined as the proper person to control finances she is bound to pay more bills and buy more items than she does if money is seen as a male responsibility. On the other hand, if shopping and paying bills is seen as a female responsibility this is likely to mean that she has greater overall control.

As we have seen, there are correlations between the financial arrangements adopted by a couple and a range of other variables, many of which are, of course, related to each other. For some couples psychological characteristics appear to dominate: money is controlled by the person with the greatest financial skills. However, being defined as having financial skills can itself be the product of ideological assumptions about the nature of femininity or masculinity. For other couples practicalities appear to dominate, with bills being paid by whoever can get to the bank, or by the partner whose earnings go monthly into the bank rather than by the one who is paid weekly in cash. However, working hours and forms of payment themselves reflect economic forces and social status.

It is not always clear what is cause and what is effect. Thus, in one

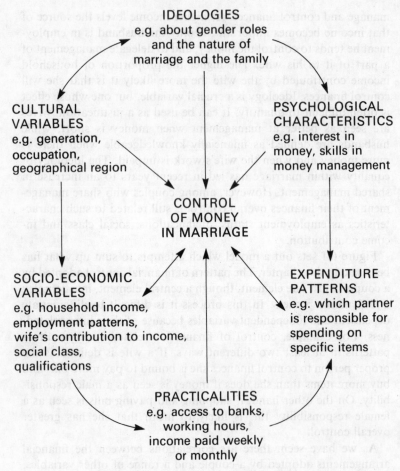

Figure 6.1   *Money and marriage: a model*

instance, the fact that a wife earns in her own right can give her more
control of household finances, while in another instance her husband's control of money can force a wife to take paid employment in
order to give her financial resources of her own. Different generations and different geographical regions also have characteristic
patterns of allocation of money: these appear as 'cultural variables'
in Figure 6.1, but they are closely related to ideology. The inter-
relationships between ideology, power in marriage and the control

of money are extremely complex. Ideology itself is fundamental. Having power in marriage can be the product of an ideology which sees power as a 'natural' attribute of men; on the other hand a man who already has power, perhaps through greater earning capacity, is also in a position to shape ideologies about the nature of marriage. Similarly, while having power can lead to one partner playing a more dominant role in money management, once that spouse has greater financial control this can in itself give him or her more power in the marriage.

7
Earning and spending

Earning money and spending money are rather different experiences, with different social meanings. Both are full of contradictions. To earn money is 'to gain by labour; to deserve'; it implies reward for hard work and entitlement to that reward and it derives from the old English word meaning 'to reap' (Chambers, 1952). Yet earning can also be seen as loss: workers contribute their labour power, in the form of time, energy and skill, receiving in exchange a wage which may barely compensate for what has been taken from them. To spend money is 'to give, bestow, to consume, to use up; to exhaust; to waste'; it implies loss and diminution (Chambers, 1952). Yet to spend is also to gain, in the form of the necessities or luxuries of daily life, and spending, too, is often hard work, though work which is normally unpaid.

Looked at from one point of view both earning and spending are stages in a conversion process. In a non-money economy one farmer may help another in exchange for a share of the produce, a cobbler and a weaver may exchange shoes for cloth, and one parent may mind another's child in exchange for help with other domestic work. The development of a money economy involves the insertion of a medium of exchange, in the form of tokens, cash or credit, into the process of converting one form of goods into another. The extent to which a money economy exists varies from one society to another. In no society are all exchanges monetarised, but no society completely lacks a medium of exchange.

Yet earning and spending have moral overtones in a way which belies the view that they are simple stages in an economic conversion process. In British society, at least, moral superiority attaches to

124

earning money in a way which stigmatises those who cannot, or do not earn. Spending money, on the other hand, is distinctly less morally virtuous, despite the hard work involved in shopping for food and household goods. The imperatives of capitalism require both production and consumption, both earning and spending, yet the inheritors of the Protestant tradition cannot seem to avoid giving moral superiority to the former. In the following pages we explore these ambiguities, drawing on the experiences and opinions of the couples who took part in the study.

Her money, his money, our money

Conflicting ideologies surround earned money. On the one hand, there is the individualistic approach represented by the statement 'It's my money: I can do what I like with it', while on the other hand, there is the assumption that the family is an economic unit. Being a breadwinner is often regarded as a burden, but it can also be a source of pride and power. Income contributed by wives keeps thousands of British families out of poverty, but wives' earnings are often still regarded as 'pin money' for 'extras'. Exploring the meanings attached to money once it enters particular households can help to elucidate these apparent contradictions.

Do married people keep their partners in ignorance of how much they earn? It seems that this practice was more widespread in the past than it is today. A number of family budget studies carried out in the first half of the twentieth century showed that it was quite common for men not to disclose their earnings, mainly so that wives should not know how much husbands kept back for themselves (Young, 1952). Gorer estimated that more than one wife in six who received a housekeeping allowance did not know how much her husband earned (Gorer, 1971, p. 92). However, more recent research has suggested that though many wives still do not know exactly how much their husbands earn most have an approximate idea, or could find out if they wanted to, for example, by looking at the bank statement or pay cheque (Wilson, 1987, p. 84).

What evidence did this study contribute to the debate? Interviewing husband and wife separately provided an opportunity to find out precisely how much each knew about the other's financial position, not just by asking whether he or she knew their partner's earnings, but by asking what those earnings were and checking against the other's answer. As far as earnings from the main job were concerned, the majority knew, either exactly or approximately, how much the other earned. However, 16 per cent of wives and 32 per cent of husbands did not know the size of their partner's income, if he or she had an income from paid work. Most of these wives, and all these husbands, said either that they could find out if they wanted to or that they had known once but had forgotten. Out of the 102 couples only three husbands kept their earnings secret from their wives.

The position was very different, however, for income from second jobs, work 'on the side' or in the black economy. Fourteen wives and 39 husbands had income from these sources. These earnings were much more likely to be kept secret: half the husbands and two-thirds of the wives whose partners had extra income of this sort did not know how much was involved. It seemed that earnings from the informal economy belonged to the individual much more firmly than did earnings from the formal economy.

Does the money belong to the person who earned it or to the family for whom it will be spent? Table 7.1 shows the answers which husband and wife, being interviewed at the same time but in different rooms, gave to the question, 'How do you feel about what you earn: do you feel it is your income or do you regard it as your husband/wife's as well?' Many respondents amended the question, explaining that they saw their main income as belonging to 'the family', rather than to themselves as a couple. There were substantial differences between husbands and wives on this issue, and also between answers relating to the income of the respondent and the income of the other partner. Men's income was more likely to be seen as pertaining to the family than was women's income. However, both men and women were more likely to see their partner's income as belonging to the individual, while they preferred to see their own income as belonging to the family as a whole. A very similar pattern was found in Australia by Edwards (1981).

The evidence presented in Table 7.1 is very relevant to the debate about the extent to which members of families see themselves as individuals or as part of a collectivity within which money is shared. First, both partners in general appear to operate a collective rather than an individualistic model of the family and to see sharing of income as the norm. Secondly, both tend to see the husband as the

Table 7.1 *'How do you feel about what you earn: do you feel it is your income or do you regard it as your husband/wife's as well?'*

| | Husband's income | | Wife's income | |
Income belongs to:	Husband's answer %	Wife's answer %	Wife's answer %	Husband's answer %
the earner	7	24	35	52
the couple/family	93	76	65	48
Total percent	100	100	100	100
Total number	99	100	52	56

main earner, the breadwinner whose income should be devoted to the needs of the family, in contrast to the wife whose earnings are seen as more marginal. Thirdly, we must note the minority of earners who see their income as their own, a minority which would probably have been larger had the interviews not been specifically focused on the issue of money management. Finally, it is interesting to see that both partners assume a higher degree of collectivity, in the form of income sharing, for themselves than for their spouse; this suggests that earners welcome the role of breadwinner and the self esteem it entails. The more frequent attribution of the breadwinner role to men reflects partly the desirability of this role and partly the larger wages men are typically able to command and the freedom from responsibility for child care which facilitates continuity of employment. In 1984 the average gross earnings of full time female employees was 66 per cent of the average earnings of male employees (Central Statistical Office, 1986). Being a breadwinner can bring privileges: the wife of an accountant, who had herself been an accounts clerk before having children, said,

> His income is his. I respect him as the worker. It's our money, but if he was really against something I would go along with him – its him that has to go to work to earn it.

In several interviews it appeared that the husband was trying to convince his wife that his income was really hers as well, but the sharing ideology being promoted by husbands tended to be received with some scepticism by wives. The difficulty which some women experience in regarding their husband's income as their own, even when encouraged to do so, was also noted by Cragg and Dawson (1984). Thus two other women said,

> He would like me to regard it as ours but I feel it is his.

> Now I regard it as mine as well, but I think it has taken a long time to feel like that – and him as well.

Perhaps one reason why some wives were reluctant to see their husbands' incomes as shared was because this idea was often linked with an ideology in which the husband's sharing of money was seen as a reward for the wife's domestic work, while her earnings were seen as outside the system. A milkman, whose wife worked part time as a nursing auxiliary said,

> Her earnings are hers. A woman cooks, cleans, dusts – she ought to be able to get a bit of pin money after looking after us ungrateful lot!

A warehouseman, whose wife did a paid job washing up, said

> Hers. What she does with her money is up to her. The work she does in the home is enough – I keep the roof over our heads. Its up to her if she works or not.

A nurse, who kept her earnings separate from those of her factory worker husband, said of her husband,

> He likes to think he is still running the house and is the breadwinner and my job is just an extra thing that I do because I want to

Yet this couple had already agreed, in the joint interview, that her earnings were used to pay the bills for the telephone, the purchase and running costs of the car, hire purchase commitments, and clothes for the wife, the husband and their three children.

Wives' earnings

What, in practice, did wives do with the money they earned? At the time of the interviews half of the women in the sample were earning and a few others had recently been in employment, so information about what wives did with their earnings was collected from 53 couples. The great majority of women made their wages available for household consumption. Of the 53, 21 placed their earnings in a joint account or in a common pool, another 13 added their wages to the housekeeping money and four used their earnings for specific bills, such as those for fuel, milk or television. Ten other women described their earnings as being for 'extras' or 'luxuries', mentioning holidays, clothes, consumer goods or improvements to the house as the sorts of items on which their money was spent. Only five wives kept their money separate from the rest of the household income and only one of these saw her earnings as her personal spending money.

These results are very similar to those of other research. For example, Morris' study in north-east England documented the decline of the 'family wage' and the increasing significance of women's earnings; however, the fact that wives typically added their wages to the housekeeping had the effect of making their economic contribution invisible (Morris, 1987). A review of the links between household finance management and labour market behaviour concluded:

> Two general patterns are apparent in the data on married women's financial attitudes and the use of the woman's wage. One is a marked desire for independence ... the other is the overwhelming tendency for women to use their wage to augment housekeeping (Morris and Ruane, 1986, p. 84).

A national survey of women's employment documented the varied reasons women give for taking paid work. When asked their main reason for working 35 per cent of women said they worked for money for basic essentials, 20 per cent worked for money for extras, while 14 per cent worked to have some money of their own. Other reasons included, for enjoyment, for company and to follow a career. Thus financial motives were predominant (Martin and Roberts, 1984, p. 68). This confirms the finding of other studies that women's earnings often play a vital part in keeping families above the official poverty line (Hamill, 1979). In the study described in this book there was a negative correlation between the husband's income and the wife's income. This meant that a lower income on the part of the man was associated with a higher income on the part of the woman and *vice versa*. In other words, if one partner had a relatively low income, the other was compensating by earning more (see appendix 2).

Earning was important to wives, both because their families needed the money and because of the independence and self esteem it brought them. Two-thirds of all the women said that it was important for them to 'have some money you know is your own'. When asked 'If your husband's income were to be increased by the same amount as you now earn, would you want to go on doing paid work?', 84 per cent of earning wives said 'yes'. Thus a nurse said of her income,

> It gives you a feeling of independence – a feeling you're not absolutely reliant on your husband. You feel you're somebody – more confident.

A sales assistant in Marks and Spencers, who saw her income as her own, still commented,

> It's mine, but I'm happy to contribute to the household expenses. I like saying 'I paid for that' sometimes.

These comments suggest that being a breadwinner can be a source of great satisfaction, an idea which was borne out by Table 7.1 in which both husbands and wives tended to see their own income as being for the family, their partner's income as for the individual earner. The association between contributing money to the household and having power in household decision making will be discussed in chapter 9. However, it is interesting that wives who saw their earnings as being for 'the family' had more power when the couple were making decisions than did wives who saw their earnings as being for themselves as individuals.

Husbands had very different attitudes to their wives' earnings as opposed to their own. As Table 7.1 showed, 93 per cent of men saw their own earnings as belonging to the family, while only 48 per cent defined their wives' earnings in this way. There was also a contrast between how husbands and wives saw the wife's earnings: while 48 per cent of husbands said that the wife's earnings belonged to the family, 65 per cent of wives saw their earnings in this way. A salesman, whose wife worked as a fruit packer on a casual basis, described a situation which was typical of many when he said,

> I like to regard her income as hers but it usually winds up going on the family.

A miner who gave his wife a weekly housekeeping allowance, and spent much of the remainder of his earnings on alcohol and fruit machines, said,

I feel I'm delegated by the family to earn money. Her job is looking after the house and family, but she feels she has to get out of the house because of boredom. We always discuss what we've got to buy and who's going to pay for it. But her money is hers.

His wife, who said she used her earnings as a school cleaner for 'extras for the family' and most recently for new windows for the house, saw her income as belonging to them both, adding, 'if he needs a new bit for the car, I'll hand the money over'. This is an example of the process by which the earnings of wives become invisible, by being ignored as pin money, earmarked for non-essentials or absorbed into the family pot (Bird, 1979, p. 178).

The data presented in this section suggest a discrepancy between theory and practice in the attitudes of husband and wife to earned income. Both partners were likely to define the husband's income as earmarked for collective expenditure; yet in practice, as we saw in chapters 5 and 6, many husbands did not make all their income available to the family, especially in households where wives were given an allowance for housekeeping. By comparison wives' incomes tended to be defined, especially by husbands, as earmarked for individual expenditure; yet in practice most wives used their income to buy things for the family, or added their earnings to the housekeeping money.

Housekeeping money

The term 'housekeeping money' here means the sum of money which is earmarked, explicitly or implicitly, for day-to-day living expenses, and especially for food, cleaning materials and so on. However, there can be a degree of ambiguity about the term because of variations in the range of goods on which it is supposed to be spent. Sometimes the word 'housekeeping' or 'housekeeping allowance' is used for all the money which husbands transfer to wives: when this is the case the housekeeping money may have to cover rent, fuel bills and clothes, as well as food. A national survey of finances asked respondents to identify the items which were paid for out of wives' housekeeping money. The following were the items mentioned: food in 100 per cent of cases; cleaning materials 88 per cent; personal things 74 per cent; newspapers and magazines 68 per cent; laundry and dry cleaning 50 per cent; insurance 50 per cent; shoe repairs 48 per cent; fuel bills 48 per cent (Young, 1977, p. 231).

There has been concern about the extent to which housekeeping money keeps pace with increases in prices and incomes and several studies were carried out on this topic in the early 1970s, when inflation was particularly high in Britain. In general it appeared that housekeeping was rising as fast as, or in some cases faster than, wages and salaries (Daniel, 1975; National Consumer Council, 1975; Young, 1977). However, all the studies revealed a substantial minority of cases in which there was a lag between, on the one hand, increases in incomes and prices and, on the other hand, increases in the amounts which husbands were giving wives for housekeeping expenses. This lag was particularly likely to occur where the husband's wages were low. A survey of poverty in London showed that 48 per cent of wives had not had any increase in their housekeeping money over the previous year, despite high inflation and rising incomes (Syson and Young, 1974). The National Consumer Council's survey concluded,

> More than one out of every four husbands (28 per cent) did not increase his housekeeping allowance at all ... the lower the income of the husband, the more likely was the wife to be kept short. Well over half the husbands earning less than £20 per week had added nothing to housekeeping money during the year. Even amongst the highest paid considerable minorities had not increased their housekeeping allowances (National Consumer Council, 1975, p. 6).

The relationship between income and housekeeping money is a crucial issue. Some of those who have written on this topic, and particularly those writing in the nineteenth century or in the first half of the twentieth century, have presented the husband's transfer of housekeeping money to his wife as the main form of intra-household reallocation. This was probably because at that time the two most common patterns of money management were the whole wage system and the allowance system, so that the husband either gave his wife all or almost all of his earnings, or he gave a fixed housekeeping allowance on a regular basis. The growth of pooling has complicated the nature of intra-household transfers, but the relationship between income and housekeeping money continues to be a central issue, and one which was explored in detail in this study.

The relationship between income and housekeeping money

Both husband and wife were asked 'Do you have a set amount that you budget for housekeeping expenses/for food and day-to-day expenses?' Half the couples who took part in the study said that they had a specific sum which they earmarked in this way, while most of the rest could name an approximate amount. Two wives and 15 husbands said that they did not know how much was spent on housekeeping, so for these couples the other partner's answer was used for the analysis. A comparison between the answers given by husbands and wives showed that the two were closely related and that when there was a discrepancy the wife was likely to give a higher figure than the husband.

On average the sum spent on housekeeping represented 26 per cent of household income. However, the proportion of total income going to housekeeping varied from 6 per cent to 75 per cent: this enormous range suggested that there might be some cases where either 'income' or 'housekeeping' had been misrepresented. Looking at the extreme cases showed that this was indeed so. Some were self-employed people whose official incomes were very low, so that practically all their earnings appeared to go as housekeeping. Others were affluent couples with substantial incomes who, in giving a sum for weekly housekeeping forgot to include the butcher's monthly bill or the cheques which they wrote at the end of bulk shopping expeditions to the supermarket: this made the sum given for housekeeping appear a ludicrously small proportion of their total income. These exceptional cases contorted the results in a misleading way, so eight couples were removed from the sample for this analysis.

Among the remaining 94 couples the average amount spent on housekeeping was £41 and the amounts spent varied from £20 to £80; these figures are very similar to those found in a study carried out in London at about the same date (Wilson, 1987, p. 121). Other comparable figures come from two national surveys carried out by market research firms. The Bird's Eye Housekeeping Monitor for

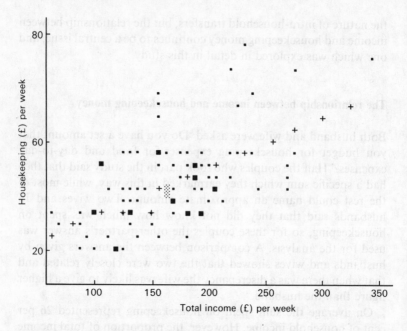

Figure 7.1   *The amount spent on housekeeping by the total income of the household*

1983 gave £53.94 as the average amount spent on housekeeping by British families, while in a survey by Millward Brown the average housekeeping was £48.70 (Bird's Eye, 1983; Nelson, 1983). The lower average figures given by the couples in Kent may reflect the wording of the questions on this topic. They were asked about 'housekeeping', but the interviewers went on to clarify what was meant by this by adding 'food and day-to-day living expenses'. This may have led some respondents to omit some bills from the figure they gave in the interview. The couples in the study spent on average 26 per cent of their income on housekeeping; this can be compared with the average British household which spent 23 per cent of its income on food in 1980 (Office of Population Censuses and Surveys, 1984).

What was the relationship between a couple's total income and the amount they spent on housekeeping? Since wives were responsible for shopping for food their estimate of housekeeping seemed to provide the most reliable figure. Figure 7.1, which plots the total

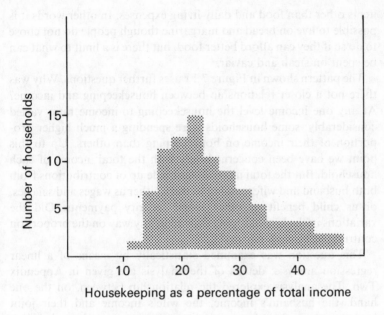

Figure 7.2 *Ratio of housekeeping to total household income*

income of the household against the wife's estimate of housekeeping, shows that in general there was a positive linear relationship between these two. As household income rose the amount spent on housekeeping increased.

However, the ratio between housekeeping and income was not the same at every income level. That is to say, though the average household spent 26 per cent of its income on housekeeping, poorer households spent a higher proportion than this, while richer households spent a lower proportion. The ratio between housekeeping and total income varied from 48 per cent in a very poor household with numerous children to 14 per cent in an affluent household with low living costs. Figure 7.2 plots the distribution of the ratios between housekeeping and income. It shows a gradual decrease in the ratio through the lower income levels and then a relatively sharp decrease at higher income levels. Figure 7.2 suggests that poor couples are able to make considerable economies in the amounts they spend, but that at higher income levels the extra money goes on items other than food and daily living expenses. In other words it is possible to live on bread and margarine though people do not chose to do so if they can afford better food, but there is a limit to what can be spent on steak and caviar.

The pattern shown in Figure 7.1 raises further questions. Why was there not a closer relationship between housekeeping and income? At any one income level the housekeeping-to-income ratio varied considerably: some households were spending a much higher proportion of their income on housekeeping than others. Up to this point we have been concerned only with the total income of each household. But the total income was made up of contributions from both husband and wife, coming to them either as wages and salaries, or as child benefit or other social security payments. Did the variations in the housekeeping depend in any way on the proportion contributed by each partner?

This question was examined statistically by means of a linear regression analysis; details of the analysis are given in Appendix Two. The analysis explored the relationship between, on the one hand, the husband's income, the wife's income and their joint income and, on the other hand, the amount spent on housekeeping. The first step was to examine the relationship between the husband's income and housekeeping. As might be expected, the analysis showed a positive relationship, in that as the husband's income increased the amount spent on housekeeping also increased.

The next step was to examine the relationship between the wife's income and the amount spent as housekeeping, that is to say, ignoring the contribution made by the husband. Again the analysis showed a positive and statistically significant correlation: the more a woman contributed, the more the household was likely to be spending on housekeeping. The analysis showed that if the wife's contribution rose by one standard deviation (£22) the housekeeping typically rose by £4.14. However, if the husband's income rose by £22 the housekeeping typically increased by only £2.70.

The third step involved adding together the incomes of husband and wife in order to explore the relationship between their total income and housekeeping. The relationship was again positive with an increase in its statistical significance. The results showed that 34 per cent of the variation in housekeeping monies could be explained by variations in total income, 19 per cent by variations in the husband's income and 9 per cent by variations in the wife's income:

these differences are mainly the product of the much larger sums earned by husbands.

Finally, a multiple regression analysis was used to examine the husband's income, the wife's income and the amount spent on housekeeping together, in order to assess the relative contribution which each income producer made to housekeeping. This analysis showed that 38 per cent of the variance in housekeeping could be attributed to variations in the husband and wife's incomes and that the relationship between housekeeping and the two forms of income, taken separately but considered together was highly significant. If the husband's income rose by one standard deviation (£48), while the wife's income was held constant, the amount spent on housekeeping would typically rise by £7.50. On the other hand, if the husband's income was held constant, while the wife's income rose by one standard deviation (£22) then housekeeping typically rose by £6.16.

In conclusion, this analysis has shown that the amount spent on housekeeping was related both to the level of household income and to the amount contributed by each partner. The regression analysis suggested that

(a) the husband contributed most absolutely to housekeeping since on average his income was four times as great as that of his wife.

(b) the wife contributed most relatively to housekeeping; this meant that if the incomes of wife and husband rose by the same amount 28 per cent of her increase would go to housekeeping compared with 16 per cent of his.

Put simply, if a pound entered the household economy through the mother's hands more of it would be spent on food for the family than would be the case if the pound had been brought into the household by the father.

We have seen that the amount spent on housekeeping was likely to differ depending on who earned the money: did it also differ according to who controlled the family's finances? Table 7.2 suggests that the way in which household finances were organised, and the person who controlled the money, had a powerful influence on the housekeeping ratio, that is on the proportion of total income spent as housekeeping. Where wives controlled finances the housekeeping

138 Money and Marriage

ratio was likely to be higher than in households where husbands controlled finances. Thus at one extreme, in wife-controlled systems, two-thirds of couples spent over a quarter of total household income on housekeeping; at the other extreme, in husband-controlled systems, only two-fifths of couples spent more than a quarter of their total income on housekeeping. This difference was statistically significant.

The same pattern existed for the mean housekeeping ratio, that is for the average proportion of income going to housekeeping. As Table 7.2 shows, the ratio was nearly a third in households where women controlled finances but only one quarter where men were in control. However, some of this difference probably reflected differences in income levels. As we have seen, housekeeping ratios are lower at higher income levels and Table 7.2 shows mean incomes increasing from £124 per week where wives controlled finances to £173 where husbands were in control.

The conclusion of this analysis is that the amount spent on housekeeping is related, first, to the level of household income, secondly, to the sources of that income and thirdly, to the control of income within the household. This pattern is very similar to that found in the important but unpublished study by MacLeod. He showed that as the net income of husbands increased the proportion of that income paid to wives for household spending decreased. Where couples managed the finances jointly a higher proportion of total income was devoted to collective expenditure than was the case when the husband retained control and gave his wife an allowance (MacLeod, 1977).

Table 7.2 *Spending on housekeeping by control of household finances*

Housekeeping ratio	Wife control	Wife-controlled pooling	Husband-controlled pooling	Husband control
Low (less than 0.25)	5	9	21	11
High (0.25 and over)	9	18	15	8
Mean housekeeping ratio	0.32	0.29	0.26	0.26
Mean income £ p w	124	157	165	173

Note: Housekeeping ratio = $\dfrac{\text{Wife's estimate of housekeeping}}{\text{Total household income}}$

These findings have important implications for policy and especially for income maintenance schemes aimed at providing financial support to families. Channelling payments via women is likely to be a more effective way of maintaining children at a given standard of living than channelling the same sum via men. Many qualitative studies have insisted that this is so but until now there has been little or no quantitative analysis available to provide confirmation.

Negotiating the housekeeping money

Many couples found it difficult to be precise about how the amount spent on housekeeping was determined. Indeed, in many households it was not determined at all, the word 'housekeeping' was rarely used and it appeared, if at all, as a retrospective concept describing the money which had been spent on food. As one husband said, when asked how they decided how much to spend on housekeeping, 'The girl at the checkout tells you what it comes to'. At the other extreme about a quarter of households kept careful accounts and had a clear notion of how much should be spent each week or month on particular items.

Table 7.3 shows four different ways in which couples made the decision about how much to spend. The most common method was for the wife to decide what was appropriate, or to buy what she considered necessary: nearly half the couples fell into this category. By definition, wives who managed household finances were responsible for deciding how much of the income should go on housekeep-

Table 7.3 *Decision about amount of housekeeping by system of money management*

| Housekeeping decided by | System of money management | | | |
	Wife management	Allowance system	Shared management	Independent management
Wife	9	–	29	4
Shared decision	–	2	13	1
Husband	–	19	13	4
Poverty controls the decision	5	1	2	–
Total number	14	22	57	9

ing, but this system was also common among couples who shared management. Here wives simply took a given sum of money from the pool every week, raising it to keep in line with wage and price increases, or in response to particular needs, often without consulting their husbands. As a lorry driver commented 'Why should a husband decide what a wife has for housekeeping when she knows the prices?'.

For at least eight of the couples the amount spent as housekeeping was severely limited by their poverty. Unlike those affluent households who simply bought what they wanted and called the money they had spent 'housekeeping', these poverty-stricken couples usually budgeted carefully, paying their bills for rent and fuel first and using what was left as economically as possible. One husband, unemployed himself and with an unemployed wife, replied to the question 'How do you decide how much to spend on housekeeping?'

> It's what's left after paying the bills really! We pay out for the bills and then the rest is housekeeping. As soon as we get the Giro cashed we walk straight over to the Rent Office to pay the rent. Then we'll go and spend a maximum of five pounds on the groceries. We are very, very careful. You've never got no money for what they call bargain offers – you can't just snap something up. I haven't bought no clothes for two and a half years – since I finished work. Same for the wife. There's no money for her to go off and buy clothes. You can never just look at something and buy it. Never.

At this income level there is no leeway for anyone to 'decide' how much to spend on housekeeping.

In other households the amount spent on housekeeping was decided by the husband, or was negotiated between husband and wife. A third of the couples in the study fell into this category. Some husbands controlled the money tightly, which could force their wives into adopting a variety of strategies when it became impossible to feed the family on the money provided. One wife with three teenage children and an unemployed husband answered the question 'How do you decide how much to spend on housekeeping?'

> We didn't decide. It was just what he gave me. It used to be £10 till a year ago. Then my daughters got on to my husband. We kept rowing, we have more rows over money than anything else. Eventually he gave in. I'd asked him before but he'd taken no notice. He raised it another £10 so now I get £20. It's like getting blood out of a stone, getting money out of him.

This money, together with £16 contributed by the eldest daughter and £5.85 child benefit, had to cover food, pocket money, presents, dog food, gas bills, cleaning materials and clothing for a household of five people. When asked what she did if the money ran out she said,

It always runs out. I've found I've got to be very, very careful what I buy. I make a shopping list and buy just those things but it still mounts up. I ask my husband for more but he often says no. If I don't get any more I go without myself. I live from hand to mouth.

When her husband was asked why they organised their finances as they did, he was unable to reply: he clearly had never considered any other method. When asked the advantages of their financial arrangements, he said

It works out so that you always have a bit left. I don't want to run out so this system ensures there's always a bit left over at the end.

The secrecy which surrounds marital finances served to maintain great inequalities between couples. Many wives who had to cajole or beg to get an increase in the housekeeping money were unaware that other wives were not forced into these sorts of strategies. These wide variations were revealed in answers to the question 'How do you go about getting an increase in the housekeeping?'. One wife replied 'I just have to ask, like most women. He'll cough up in the end'. The wife of a technical services manager said she got a rise,

By rowing. The present amount was decided eight months ago. My husband did the shopping for one month and decided the amount. There should be government legislation about how much housekeeping should be.

Her husband's answer was rather different. He said housekeeping money was decided,

By mutual agreement, with an eye to what we can afford. She would like more and I would like her to have less because we just don't have it. I know it's not enough.

One wife, in a couple who saw their money as pooled, explained how she negotiated an increase in the sum set aside for food:

I ask, there's no problem, but I don't like actually asking. I do choose my moment and work my way round to it. He is normally OK but he might want to complain for an hour and a half or so, but he lets me have it if I say I really need it.

All these answers are very different from those of the genuinely pooling wife who said simply 'I just go and cash more from the bank'.

Who spends on what?

What is the relationship between patterns of earning within the household and patterns of spending? Does the allocative system function as a filter which makes it more likely that one partner or the other will be responsible for spending on particular items? The relationship between patterns of earning and patterns of spending was investigated by Piachaud (1982). He argued that as married women contributed a larger share of the household income, spending might be expected to shift towards, for example, convenience foods and consumer durables. His analysis of the Family Expenditure Survey showed that this was not the case. Where a woman contributed a larger share of the household income spending on food and consumer durables was not greater, though more was spent on clothes, alcohol and tobacco. Piachaud suggested that the pressures of paid work might have led women to drink and smoke more. An alternative explanation could be that the increased contribution of the wife allowed the husband to feel free to spend more of his income on alcohol and tobacco, a phenomenon observed by Jephcott *et al.* in their study of women working in a biscuit factory in East London (1962). Piachaud concluded by acknowledging the complexity of the processes involved and the need for further research.

In making connections between earning and spending, the allocative system is a crucial intervening variable. The relationship can be expressed very simply:

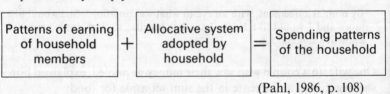

(Pahl, 1986, p. 108)

Each allocative system has different implications for purchasing behaviour. To some extent this is tautologous, since one criterion in defining allocative systems is responsibility for household expenditure. However, the other criterion, which is access to the main source of income of the household, constrains the amount of resources to which each spender has access and the freedom with which he or she can use those resources. Thus in an allowance system household the wife may be free to spend without consulting her husband, but only on those items which her allowance is intended to cover. If the allowance is inadequate for her responsibilities her spending will be reduced, even if her husband is a wealthy man. Where management of money is shared each partner may be purchasing a wider range of items, but this freedom will often be constrained by having to justify spending to the other person. Whether husband or wife has overall control of the pool is likely to determine which partner has to account for spending to the other and which has to ask before using pooled resources. The allocation of expenditure responsibilities was clearly a complex process, in which various factors played a part: these included not only the way the couple managed and controlled their finances but also gender, the level of income and the way in which income was paid.

Patterns of spending were differentiated by gender, as Table 7.4 shows. Wives were most likely to pay for food, clothing for themselves and their children, presents, and school expenses such as dinner money. Husbands were likely to be responsible for paying for their own clothing, the car, repairs and decorating, meals taken away from home, and alcohol. Joint responsibilities, paid for by either partner or after a joint decision, included consumer durables, donations to charity and Christmas expenses. This pattern is similar to that found by Todd and Jones (1972): the main difference between the two studies lies in the increase in goods purchased by 'either or both', a change which reflects the spread of joint bank accounts.

However, there were significant differences in spending patterns according to the allocative system adopted by the couple. Where wives managed the money they were usually responsible for almost all spending, with some sharing of responsibility in the areas of consumer goods, meals out and holiday expenses. On the other hand, in households with allowance systems husbands were responsible for the majority of items, leaving wives to pay for food, their own clothes and expenditure on the children. In households where

Table 7.4   *Household spending patterns*
(all percentages of total 102)

| | Person responsible for spending on each item | | | |
	Wife	Husband	Either/both	Not applicable other answers
Food	74	9	18	–
Rent/mortgage	31	35	23	11
Fuel	30	41	27	2
Telephone	28	41	10	21
House insurance	28	40	25	9
Life insurance	28	37	25	10
Clothes and shoes (wife)	78	7	15	–
Clothes and shoes (husband)	24	50	27	–
Clothes and shoes (children)	69	7	24	1
Car or motor bike	4	51	14	31
School expenses	63	10	13	15
Repairs and decorating	14	58	28	1
Consumer goods	12	41	42	5
Children's pocket money	27	16	27	31
Presents	61	2	36	1
Meals out/trips out	4	60	23	13
Papers/books	49	23	21	8
Holiday expenses	10	38	35	17
Charities	43	4	48	5
Christmas expenses	44	5	50	1
Drinks in house	13	36	15	37
Drinks in pub	2	55	9	34

management was shared responsibilities were more equally divided, with many areas of spending in which either partner could pay, so that a particular bill might be paid out of a joint account or might fall to the wife on one occasion and to the husband on another. Couples who managed their finances independently tended to allocate major bills to the husband and food spending to the wife, while sharing responsibility for presents, meals out, holidays, donations to charity and spending on Christmas.

Whether spending patterns differed according to how the couple managed their money depended partly on the item purchased. For some items of expenditure there was a relationship between who paid the bill and how the couple managed their money; however, for other items who paid the bill did not differ according to the system of money management. There was a significant relationship between responsibility for spending and the system of money management for the following items: rent or mortgage, rates, fuel, house insurance, life insurance, the husband's clothes, car purchases, running costs of car, school expenses, consumer goods, meals out. For all the other items listed in Table 7.4 money management was not related to expenditure pattern.

Table 7.5 shows how spending patterns can vary according to different allocative systems, taking spending on fuel as an example. It shows that in two-fifths of households husbands were responsible for fuel bills compared with a third of households where wives paid for gas, coal and electricity: thus though in general husbands were more likely than wives to be responsible for fuel bills, the difference was not great. There were striking differences however, between allowance system couples, where two-thirds of fuel bills were paid by husbands, and wife-managed systems where nearly all fuel bills were paid by wives. This last finding has important implications for all who are concerned about fuel poverty. Since households where wives manage all the money are among the poorest households, wives are likely to be the ones who struggle to pay fuel bills out of inadequate incomes (Bradshaw and Harris, 1983; Parker, 1987).

Spending on rent or mortgage showed the same pattern. The wife was responsible for this payment in households with a whole wage system, while the husband was usually responsible in households with an allowance system or with independent management of money. In households with shared management of money the pattern was more complex. However, if these couples were divided between wife-controlled pooling, and husband-controlled pooling, the wife typically paid the rent or mortgage in the former group

Table 7.5 *Responsibility for fuel bills by system of money management*

Fuel bill paid by	All households	Wife management	Allowance system	Shared management	Independent management
Wife	31	12	2	16	1
Husband	42	0	15	22	5
Either or both	27	2	5	17	3
Other answers	2	0	0	2	0
Total number	102	14	22	57	9

while the husband was responsible for this payment in the latter group. As we saw in the last chapter, wife management and wife control of money are both associated with low household income. This means that those households which are most likely to find it hard to pay their housing costs are also those where wives are responsible for finances, even though they may not be the main earners. This has important implications for policies related to the non-payment of rent, or to foreclosure on mortgages.

Spending on leisure

Research on 'leisure' has shown that typically women and men have rather different ideas of what the term leisure means and different amounts of time and money to devote to it. As a concept 'leisure' is an imprecise term, but it tends to be seen in opposition to 'work', meaning paid employment. Used in this way leisure means time which belongs to the individual, as opposed to the time which belongs to the employer, and leisure activities are those which people choose for themselves as opposed to activities which are an obligatory part of doing a particular job. Feminists have criticised this dichotomy, arguing that particularly for married women the meaning of the term 'leisure' is much less clear than this, partly because the word 'work' is inaccurate if it is used as a synonym for paid employment (see especially Deem, 1986).

For a married woman with children 'work' includes not only paid employment but also domestic work and child care. Since the work of caring for young children involves taking responsibility for them throughout the twenty-four hours of every day, mothers of young children have no leisure time, in the sense of time which is freely available to the individual. There is a distinction between the role of mother or wife, and the tasks associated with motherhood or wifehood. For many women the roles represent twenty-four hour commitments, but the tasks can be done within circumscribed periods of time, leaving time spare for leisure. However, this is not leisure in the sense in which single people and many married men experience it, since at any time the demands of the role of mother or wife can claim priority over the woman's leisure activities.

A number of studies have shown that, compared with men, women have less 'free' time to give to leisure, see leisure and sport as much less central to their identity, are involved in fewer activities outside the home, and belong to fewer clubs and organisations; these differences are particularly pronounced among the working class and among couples with young children (Rapoport and Rapoport, 1975; Talbot, 1979; Deem, 1986). A study of leisure and gender in Sheffield showed that lack of money, and not liking to go out alone after dark, were major constraints on women's activities (Green, Hebron and Woodward, 1986). The different lifestyles of married men and married women are a reflection of the ways in which gender differences structure daily life. For women, participation in activities outside the home is often limited by the expense involved, by the disapproval of husbands, by the embarrassment and possible danger involved in going out alone at night, or by the sexism of those who provide leisure and sports facilities. On the other hand, men's leisure tends to be seen as a well-earned reward for paid work and there are few barriers to going out to participate in organised leisure activities. A study of redundancy showed that when wives become unemployed their first economy is to give up spending on themselves, while husbands typically continue to have some personal spending money, even though the amount may be reduced (Callender, 1987, p. 151).

In this study the question of spending on leisure was approached in various different ways. Each person was asked what leisure activities he or she pursued and how much was spent on each activity. Each was then asked to describe their partner's leisure pursuits and to estimate how much he or she spent on them. There were other questions about 'personal spending money'. In the joint interview each individual was asked to identify a source of money for personal things 'like cigarettes, tights, a drink out with friends, a present for your spouse'. In the separate interviews each was asked about their personal spending money, the sums involved and the items it had to cover; each was also asked about their partner's personal spending money.

In general the questions on personal spending money in the separate interview did not 'work' very well, in that many respondents denied having a sum set aside as personal spending money, despite the fact that they had identified a source of money for spending on their personal needs and had described leisure activities which cost money. The probable explanation is that most couples did not set aside specific sums for personal spending money, but yet recognised that each partner had to have a source of money for personal needs and pleasures.

Husbands were more likely to have money for personal spending and for leisure than were wives. Thus 44 per cent of husbands said that they had a sum for personal spending, compared with only 28 per cent of wives, and 86 per cent of the men spent money on leisure activities compared with 67 per cent of the women. Husbands were also likely to have more money to spend on themselves than wives. Among the 102 couples who took part in the study seven either spent nothing on leisure or had no set amounts for this, while 23 couples spent approximately the same amounts. Seventeen wives spent more than their husbands on leisure activities, while 55 husbands spent more than their wives. Estimating spending on leisure is difficult because it is often spasmodic, with subscriptions payable yearly, fees for classes payable termly, sports equipment bought when needed and so on. Nevertheless, the problem of estimating the amount spent on leisure applied to both husbands and wives, since they were asked identical sets of questions, so it may be assumed that comparisons between the two sets of answers are justified, even if the total amounts spent are likely to be inaccurate. However, it is important to remember that drinking and gambling were the most common leisure activities on which men spent money and that sums spent on these are notoriously underestimated. Thus, if anything men were spending even more on leisure than they admitted to the interviewers.

Typically, husbands over-estimated the amounts wives spent on leisure, while wives under-estimated how much their husbands spent. They also had rather different attitudes to each others' leisure activities. Both husbands and wives tended to give precedence to the husband's right to leisure: as a nurse said of her milkman husband: 'You can't deny a man when he's earning'. By contrast wives' rights to leisure seemed less secure and 'leisure' sometimes involved domestic work. Thus when one husband was asked what leisure activities his wife had, he replied, 'Ironing, sewing, reading'.

Employment status had both financial and ideological implications. Wives who were earning had more money to spend and more money over which they had a degree of control, but they also felt they had a right to pursue leisure activities of which their husbands disapproved, such as going to the pub with women friends or taking independent holidays. Unemployment could drastically alter leisure patterns. One couple said,

> Husband: I used to spend money on the garden when I was at work but I can't now. There's a twenty foot greenhouse in the garden and its empty. No money for seeds or anything like that.

> Wife: I used to play bingo, but we can't afford it. I like to read but I borrow books from friends. I like a Mills and Boon in bed.

An unemployed sheet metal worker had turned his hobby into a form of self provisioning.

> I go fishing at night. I borrow my father's car, he puts the petrol in and I dig my own bait. I go to Dover or Sandwich. I've got a freezer full of cod: its a good meal, cod, full of protein. I used to be on my own down there, but now its packed, even in the middle of the night. People get so bored being unemployed, and it makes a break, going fishing.

The fact that a wife managed or controlled the money did not necessarily give her more to spend on herself. An office cleaner married to a warehouseman said:

> I work out what I need for housekeeping and work out if I can buy tights or anything else – only if I can afford it. I come last on the list. He knows I spend hardly anything on myself: he would like me to spend more, but we can't afford it.

What determined the amount of money which each person felt they could spend on leisure and personal needs? Table 7.6 shows

Table 7.6 *Sources of personal spending money*

Personal spending money taken from	Wives	Husbands
Pool or joint account	40	39
Own earnings	17	39
Housekeeping money	38	7
Separate amount for this purpose	2	12
None/other answers	5	5
Total number	102	102

from what part of the household budgeting system each person drew her or his personal spending money. Husbands were more likely than wives to take their personal spending money from their earnings, while wives were likely to use housekeeping money for their personal needs; 12 husbands, but only two wives, had a sum set aside for their personal use. The source of personal spending money varied according to how the couple organised their finances. Where there was a joint account and money management was shared, both partners tended to get their own spending money from the pool. When money was managed independently both partners took their personal spending money from their earnings. Where there was an allowance system the husband's personal spending money tended to come from his earnings, while the wife's money came from the housekeeping money, a situation which was particularly likely to make a woman feel that she had no right to spend on herself. This point was made vividly by the sociologist Lee Comer:

> If any sociologist . . . had inquired into the financial arrangements in my marriage I would have laid my hand on my heart and sworn that we shared money equally. And in theory I would have been telling the truth. In fact it would have no more occurred to me to spend money on anything but housekeeping than it would for him not to (Comer, 1974, p. 124).

The ideological construction of the relationship between earner and dependant, which expresses itself in the dependant's deference and subordination, is seen particularly clearly in the case of spending on personal needs and leisure.

Table 7.7 shows how spending on leisure varied depending on how a couple managed their money. In the sample as a whole husbands were likely to spend more than their wives, but this was especially so when money was managed by the wife or managed independently. Thus in households where wives managed the money only one wife, but ten husbands, spent more on leisure than their partners. Among couples who shared the management of money 12 wives and 24 husbands spent more than their partners. The pattern was similar when couples were divided according to the typology of control of finances. When wives controlled finances, and there was no joint account, husbands were typically spending more than wives on leisure. An unexpected result was found, however, when wife-controlled pooling couples were compared with husband-controlled

Table 7.7 *Amounts spent on leisure by system of money management*

| Leisure spending | *System of money management* | | | |
	Wife management	Allowance system	Shared management	Independent management
Husband more than wife	10	13	25	7
Approximately equal amounts	3	6	20	1
Wife more than husband	1	3	12	1
Total number	14	22	57	9

pooling couples. It was among the latter category that wives who spent more on leisure than their husbands were most commonly found. Of the 17 women who spent more on leisure than their husbands, ten were found in those households where the husband controlled finances and there was a joint account.

Conclusion

This chapter has attempted to clarify some of the complicated social processes which determine the uses to which money is put as it passes from earners to spenders within the household. Who earns the money, and who controls and manages it, all have an impact on patterns of expenditure. It is important to recognise that expenditure is not the same as consumption. Knowing who buys a particular item, or what was bought, does not necessarily tell us who consumed that item. Equally, knowing a household's income does not necessarily tell us much about patterns of expenditure: there may be deprived individuals within households with substantial incomes. Especially when money is short, managing resources so that they are shared as equitably as possible can be crucial in maintaining the health and well-being of individuals within families (Graham, 1984).

This chapter has presented what may be the most important findings of the study. Where wives control finances a higher proportion of household income is likely to be spent on food and day-to-day living expenses than is the case where husbands control finances; additional income brought into the household by the wife is more likely to be spent on food than additional money earned by the husband. Additional support for these hypotheses comes from the finding that husbands are likely to spend more on leisure than wives. These results have important implications for all who are concerned about the living standards of children, about the employment of women, and about tax and social security policies which affect families.

8

Income maintenance, personal taxation and family ideologies

This chapter is concerned with the involvement of the state in the financial arrangements of families. The relationship between 'the state' and 'the family' is extremely complex: even the definition of these two terms is fraught with difficulties. In an interesting discussion of this issue Morgan defines the state as 'all those institutions, categories of persons and individuals who are involved in the financing and administration of legislation ... governments and ministries, the civil service, the judiciary, the police, professionals working in the public sector, and so on' (Morgan, 1985, p. 65). The state has a multi-dimensional impact on families, for example, in the regulation of births and deaths, through legislation relating to education, taxation, income maintenance, divorce and inheritance, and by the help it provides (or does not provide) for dependent members of families. Families contribute to the state through the production and reproduction of the labour force, through caring for dependants and through the maintenance of familial ideologies promoting forms of family life which serve the interests of the state. In this chapter we consider state policies concerned with providing financial support for dependent children and those who care for them, and we examine the ideological implications of different strategies.

There are many different methods, and combinations of methods, by which tax and income maintenance systems make provision for the financial support of children. This chapter examines two particular policy options, but these should be seen as examples illustrating a more general theoretical debate. Financial support can be given to mothers or to fathers, or to them jointly; it can be given as

reductions in taxation, or as cash handouts in the form of social
security payments or tax credits; it can come through the state in the
form of tax or social security, or through employment, in the form of
workplace nurseries, child bonuses on wages or parental leave. It is
important to recognise that any one policy reflects value judgements
about the nature of family life and about the social and economic
ordering of society. There is never a single 'best' policy but only
policies which are best in terms of a particular ideology (for an
extended discussion see Edwards, 1981a and 1984).

Giving financial support to fathers maintains the position of the
male as head of the family and as the breadwinner who is responsible
for 'his' wife and children. On the other hand, giving financial
support to mothers is likely to strengthen the position of women
within the family and to improve the standard of living of women
and children, especially in households where male earners do not
share their income with non-earners. This debate was expressed
most cogently by Eleanor Rathbone in her pioneering work, *The
Disinherited Family*. Her book argued the case for financial support
for dependent children, which she termed Family Endowment, and
began,

> I doubt whether there is any subject in the world of equal importance that
> has received so little serious and articulate consideration as the economic
> status of the family – of its members in relation to each other and of the
> whole unit in relation to the other units of which the community is made
> up (Rathbone, 1924, p. vii).

Rathbone set out the arguments of those who continued to oppose
giving financial help to families with children.

> It is assumed in these appeals that the beauty of the tie between husband
> and wife, father and child, will be impaired and its strength weakened, if
> there is anything less than complete financial dependency. It is further
> assumed that the father's motive to industry will be undermined if he no
> longer feels that he stands between his children and starvation (Rathbone,
> 1924, p. 248).

She concluded her case for Family Endowments with the words,

> Nothing can justify the subordination of one group of producers – the
> mothers – to the rest, and their deprivation of all share of their own in the

wealth of a community which depends on them for its very existence (Rathbone, 1924, p. 274).

These quotations make it clear that the debate about how financial help should be provided for families with dependent children raises fundamental ideological issues about, for example, work incentives, the value of unpaid work in the home, and the nature of relationships between women and men, and between parents and children.

Whether financial support is given in the form of tax allowances or social security payments raises another set of issues. On the one hand, it has been argued that recipients may see receiving social security payments as stigmatising by comparison with receiving the same amount as earned income from which tax has not been deducted. On the other hand tax allowances, appearing in the form of a larger wage packet or salary cheque, may seem less tangible than a cashable money order from social security. This difference is reflected at the macro-economic level. The system of public accounts used in Britain is such that tax allowances do not appear as public expenditure, while social security is the largest single item in the government's annual expenditure plan. This has significant implications. For example, abolishing the married man's tax allowance would currently release over £4 billion, a sum which would make it possible to double the level of child benefit. However, the effect of this change would be to increase spending on social security by 10 per cent, while the increased income accruing to the Inland Revenue would appear in a different, and less politically sensitive part of the national accounts.

It is impossible to isolate families from the social and economic context in which they are located: inequalities in the wider society are translated into inequalities within the family, and *vice versa*. Social and economic policy plays a crucial part in this process, whether by reinforcing patterns of inequality or by compensating for structural inequalities. Land made this point in her study of the introduction of child benefit, then known as family allowances. She suggested that family allowances were supported in the early days as a means of reducing inequalities between rich and poor, and between men and women. To socialists and feminists these were worthy ends in themselves but they were not regarded as legitimate ends for government social policy until the Second World War. Broader support from Liberals and Conservatives was forthcoming only when family allowances became linked with other problems: a declining birth rate, poverty and malnutrition among children, the maintenance of work incentives and the need to curb inflation. These problems were established concerns of government and thus, by association, the legitimacy of family allowances was enhanced (Land, 1975, p. 227).

The state, through legislation, has a profound effect on the balance of power within families. Legislation which grants a benefit to one parent rather than another shifts the balance in terms of how much each contributes to the family budget and how much spending power each partner controls. Legislation which treats husband and wife as individuals can have a very different impact from that which treats them as a unit. A particular policy can enshrine existing gender roles or can open the way to new patterns of gender relationships. Conversely, the changing nature of family life is reflected in changes in social and economic policy. Examining proposed changes in policies for income maintenance and taxation, from the point of view both of members of families and of those who frame legislation, offers an opportunity to explore the ideologies which underlie policy alternatives.

Child benefit

This is a non-means-tested benefit payable to anyone who is responsible for a dependent child. It is normally collected by mothers from their local post office. Child benefit has been the subject of considerable public debate. Some have suggested that it should be means-tested or even abolished, while others have urged that it should be raised substantially, as a way of ameliorating poverty and sharing the costs of child rearing (Brown, 1988; Henwood and Wicks, 1986; Walsh and Lister, 1985). In 1982 four-weekly payments of child benefit were introduced and current recipients had to complete a form if they wanted to continue to receive weekly payments. New mothers now automatically get the benefit every four weeks in arrears, unless they are receiving income support, family credit or one parent benefit, or can demonstrate that four-weekly payments lead to hardship. Other possible changes which have been proposed are the payment of child benefit yearly, payment into bank accounts instead of through post offices, and means-testing before payment is made.

Politicians, pressure groups and academics have been vociferous, but little has been heard from the recipients of child benefit. How important is child benefit to families and how is it used? More precisely, what are the views of the women who each week, or month, collect the benefit on behalf of each of their children? And do the views of mothers differ from the views of fathers? This study provided an opportunity to explore some of these questions. In the interviews both husband and wife were asked a series of questions about child benefit, with the aim of investigating current use of the benefit and possible changes. In all but one of the families it was normally the wife who collected the money from the post office. Wives were asked, 'What do you usually spend child benefit on?' The majority (61 per cent) replied that the money went in with the general funds, to be spent on food and daily shopping; 32 per cent said that they kept the money specifically for things for the children; 6 per cent saved the money, most often in a children's savings account in the post office; one wife used child benefit as her personal spending money.

Next wives were asked 'How important is child benefit for you?' At the time the actual sum involved amounted to only £5.85 per child per week, and the real value of child benefit was less than at any time since it was first introduced in 1946. Nevertheless, this small sum was important to the great majority of its recipients. Only 6 per cent of the women said that it was not important to them, 49 per cent described it as important, and 45 per cent as very important. Those who said that it was not important often commented on the sum they received. A play group supervisor said,

> The amount it is, it's almost immaterial – of course it helps but it's a pathetic amount – it doesn't do much more than pay the dinner money!

> It's not nearly enough – it's a drop in the ocean – but its better than a slap in the face with a wet lettuce.

For whom was child benefit particularly important? As one would expect, wives in low income households were more likely to say that child benefit was very important. However, the association between describing child benefit as very important and having a low household income was not particularly strong. There was a much stronger association between the importance of child benefit to the wife and the system of money management used by the couple. Table 8.1 illustrates this point.

It is not surprising to see that child benefit was very important to 86 per cent of women in households where wives managed the budget since, as we have seen, these were in general the poorer households. However, Table 8.1 emphasises the value of child benefit for wives on allowance systems, none of whom described it as unimportant. Typically these households have quite high incomes, but the husband is often the only earner and gives his wife a set amount weekly or monthly with which she buys food and pays specific bills. For a wife receiving an allowance from her husband, child benefit may be the only money she can spend as she wants. A husband with relatively high earnings may fail to give his wife enough money to cover the bills which she is expected to pay: in these circumstances child benefit can acquire an importance for the wife out of all proportion to the sum involved. If child benefit were to be means-tested, and the household were chosen as the unit for the means test, these women would be deprived of a small but very significant part of their income.

Child benefit was important both as income and as spending money. As income it gave wives the feeling that they were contributing financially. One woman, caring full-time for two small children commented, 'It's the only bit of thing I contribute to the family'. As spending money it gave wives a small measure of autonomy and independence, as well as helping to pay the bills. The wife of a warehouse worker, herself currently without paid employment, said, 'It's my one thing I can fall back on, my bit of independence'. Even in households where money was pooled, wives often felt they had to account to their husbands for expenditure, especially if they were not earning themselves. One such wife said,

It's nice to have money without having to ask. It's the thing about asking, isn't it? Although really the family allowance (child benefit) is mine. We don't pool that. It's very important. It's the only source of money that I've got that I can spend how I want to.

The study also provided evidence about the changes occurring in child benefit. The interviews took place a few months after the

Table 8.1 *The importance of child benefit to the wife by system of money management*

Child benefit is	Wife management %	Allowance system %	Shared management %	Independent management %	All %
Very important	86	50	39	11	45
Important	7	50	54	78	49
Not important	7	0	7	11	6
Total per cent	100	100	100	100	100
Total number	14	22	57	9	102

transition to four-weekly payments. Since all the families were already in receipt of benefit they had the option of continuing to receive weekly payments, but had to take the positive step of filling in a form in order that this should happen. Out of the 102 couples who took part in the study, 75 per cent were receiving child benefit weekly and only 25 per cent received it four-weekly. This figure was similar to the national average: information from the Department of Health and Social Security showed that at the time when the interviews were carried out, 70 per cent of all recipients had opted to receive child benefit weekly.

Why had so many women made the effort to remain with weekly payments? There were no clear differences between the group who had chosen to go on receiving child benefit weekly and those who had changed to receiving it every four weeks. This seems to reflect the great diversity within these two groups. The questionnaire did not ask women why they had opted for weekly payments but just over half volunteered an explanation. The most common reason, volunteered by 23 women, was that all their budgeting was done on a weekly basis and that they would not be able to manage without the additional money from child benefit:

> I have to have it weekly otherwise I couldn't manage: we wouldn't eat at the moment without it.

> I've always worked on a weekly basis because everything is paid to me weekly.

The next most common reason, volunteered by 18 of the women, related to the convenience of child benefit as an accessible source of money, available if necessary to supplement the weekly budget. As one wife put it: 'You never know when you might need it'.

Answers to questions about proposed changes to child benefit revealed substantial differences between husbands and wives. When asked what they would feel if benefits were paid yearly, 71 per cent of wives said that they would dislike this compared with 57 per cent of husbands. Yearly payments of child benefit were welcomed by 16 per cent of wives and 18 per cent of husbands, though some respondents were quick to add that it would have to be paid in advance rather than in arrears; 25 per cent of husbands and 14 per cent of wives said that the change to yearly payments would not affect them or gave other answers. There were differences, too, when couples were asked about payments going into bank accounts instead of being made through post offices: 53 per cent of wives said that this would cause problems for them, as opposed to 36 per cent of husbands. One wife said,

> It would be extra hard – I would have to ensure that I got it off him – it would be hard. I would object strongly. I want control of it myself – not into a joint account!

It is sometimes suggested that we should return to giving families financial help through tax allowances on earnings rather than through specific payments to parents. Some respondents volunteered opinions on this issue, though significantly, those who did so were all men:

> I wish we didn't have it at all. I would rather have the difference in tax benefits!

> I think it should be stopped anyway. They only take it off you in tax. It would be better to be in my wage packet.

The answers to the questions on child benefit illustrate a number of themes which have run through this book. Child benefit is particularly valued, not only by women in low income households, but also by women whose husbands exercise a high degree of control over the family budget, even though the household income may be quite large. These women would lose a valued source of income if child benefit were to be means-tested and paid only to poorer families. This point underlines the importance of considering the intra-household economy in any discussion about the payment of benefits.

Clear discrepancies between the answers given by husbands and wives illustrated the differences between 'his' marriage and 'her' marriage. Most husbands saw child benefit as an insignificant part of the household income. They were less likely than their wives to reject the idea of yearly payments and more likely to suggest that the benefit should return to its original form as a child tax allowance, set against the earnings of fathers. For wives the benefit was important not only because it was an independent source of income, but also because it was paid weekly, so that it fitted in with women's responsibility for weekly budgeting for food and daily living expenses. Their comments suggested that if it were paid yearly it would be spent on different items and might be incorporated into a male-controlled part of the family budget. Child benefit is important because it represents some recognition of the hard work and financial sacrifice which child rearing involves, especially for women (Joshi, 1987). Unlike the wages system it takes account of family size, and unlike the social security system it ensures that the money goes directly to mothers. The results presented here confirm the continuing significance of child benefit, despite the paltry sums involved.

Personal taxation

Taxation is another area of policy in which assumptions are made, implicitly if not explicitly, about financial arrangements within marriage. It is also an area of policy which has been used as a way of giving financial support to children and those who care for them, for example through child tax allowances. These allowances were introduced in 1909; they were set against the earnings of fathers and their effect was to increase the take-home pay of men with children.

After family allowances were introduced in 1946 there were essentially two ways in which the state gave financial help to families with children: these were the child tax allowance, which benefited fathers who earned enough to pay tax, and the family allowance, which benefited mothers regardless of their income level. In the early

1970s it was proposed that the child tax allowance and the family allowance should both be abolished, to be replaced by a single benefit. Originally this was to be paid as a tax credit through the father's wage packet, but the proposal aroused such a storm of opposition from women, who would be losing their family allowance, that the idea had to be abandoned. Instead child benefit was introduced, to be paid to mothers. Fathers lost their child tax allowance and mothers gained an increased child allowance: the newspapers of the time commented that there had been a transfer 'from the wallet to the purse' (Brown, 1988).

However, the taxation system continued to give privileges to married men by comparison with married women. First, married men received a higher tax allowance than married women and single people. All earners are allowed a certain sum free of tax, but the married man's tax allowance has always stood at about 160 per cent of the other personal tax allowances. The existence of this special tax allowance represented support for marriage and for the particular form of marriage in which a male breadwinner supports a dependent wife. Secondly, the tax system continued to privilege married men by taxing couples as one unit and identifying the husband as that one. In the words of the Income and Corporation Taxes Act of 1970, s.37, 'A woman's income chargeable to income tax shall . . . for any year during which she is a married woman living with her husband, be deemed for income tax purposes to be his income and not to be her income'.

This ruling had its origins in the common law tradition that husband and wife were a unit, represented legally by the husband. However, as we saw in chapter 2, the Married Women's Property Acts of 1870 and 1882 entitled women to keep control of their own income and property. Why, then, did the married woman continue to be subsumed within her husband for tax purposes? The Royal Commission on Income Tax suggested that,

The aggregation for income tax purposes of the income of husband and wife is not dependent upon any medieval conception of the subordination of women . . . It is beyond question that in the immense majority of cases where the wife has separate means she contributes to the common purse, either by the actual merger of her income with her husband's or by bearing expenses which in less fortunate households would fall upon the husband (Chancellor of the Exchequer, 1980, p. 58).

The aggregation of husband and wife for tax purposes was attacked for denying women privacy and independence in financial matters and for making the assumption that married people always combine their income. As we saw in chapters 5 to 7, all couples do not pool their money, while violent husbands and men whose marriages are breaking down are particularly unlikely to share their income with their wives.

Dissatisfaction with the existing system led to pressure for reform and to the publication of two Green Papers, the first on *The Taxation of Husband and Wife* and the second on *The Reform of Personal Taxation* (Chancellor of the Exchequer, 1980 and 1986). Both Green Papers proposed the setting-up of a new structure for income tax, based on independent taxation and transferable tax allowances. Everybody was to have a tax allowance in his or her own right. Married people who could not use up all their tax allowance would be able to transfer the balance to their partners. So if, for example, a wife did not earn her allowance was to be added to that of her husband to give him a personal allowance of double that available to a single person. It was claimed that the changes would benefit couples where one partner was unable to earn because of responsibility for young children.

The proposal was criticised for a number of different reasons. First, it was argued that the transferable personal allowance would benefit couples where the husband was the sole earner, but only provided that his pay were high enough to absorb all the available tax allowances. The full benefits of the transferable tax allowance would therefore be denied to low income families.

Secondly, transferable allowances were attacked as an inefficient way of increasing the income available to families where one parent cannot earn because of responsibility for child care. Among one earner households, childless couples would in reality gain more than those with children from the change to transferable allowances. This analysis was carried out by the Institute for Fiscal Studies; the authors concluded that a more direct way of assisting households with children would be to increase child benefit (Symons and Walker, 1986). It is interesting that, among the 37 organisations who submitted evidence following the publication of *The Taxation of Husband and Wife*, only four favoured retaining existing arrangements, 13 supported a change to transferable allowances, while 20 advocated giving financial help to families with children through increasing child benefits. It was argued that this would produce a transfer of wealth from childless couples to those with children, from the older to the younger and from the higher to the lower paid (Kay and Sandler, 1982). To put the same point in another way, transferable allowances benefit all households where only one partner works (whether or not there are children or other dependants in the household). Increases in child benefit give income to all households with children (whether or not one or both partners work) (Kay, 1985, p. 68). This example illustrates the point that tax and social security policy can never be value free. Any particular policy option will benefit some at the expense of others: choosing between options involves making value judgements and these reflect particular ideological positions.

Thirdly, it was argued that transferable personal allowances would have significant effects on the employment of married women. If a wife returned to paid work after a period without earnings she would face a choice between either leaving her allowance with her husband and therefore paying tax on all of her earnings, or taking her allowance back and so subjecting her husband to additional taxation which would result in a reduction in his take home pay (Morris and Ruane, 1986, p. 21). The Green Paper suggested that the effects would be negligible, quoting the example of Denmark, which has operated a form of transferable allowances for some time and which has the highest proportion of married women in employment of any country in the European Community (Chancellor of the Exchequer, 1986, p. 15). However, researchers at the Institute of Fiscal Studies calculated that as many as 200,000 women, 3.5 per cent of all married women now in employment, would leave the labour force if transferable allowances were introduced in Britain; many others would reduce their hours of work (Dilnot, 1986).

The proposal to introduce transferable personal allowances raised fundamental issues. As a *Times* leader began 'the treatment of the family is an issue that goes to the heart of any system of income taxation' (*The Times*, 1985). The leader writer went on to argue in favour of transferable allowances, on the grounds that the system would be 'completely neutral as to whether husband, wife or both were earning the family income', and that it would 'smooth out the rise and fall in family income that follows the normal pattern in which the wife stops work to start a family and rejoins the labour force as the children reach school age'. However, the House of Lords Committee argued strongly against the transferable allowance on the grounds that, far from being neutral, it would 'create a substantial disincentive to wives seeking paid employment'. It advocated totally independent taxation of the earned incomes of husband and wife: Lady Serota, who headed the Committee, concluded that 'the issue of transferable allowances provides a crucial test of the strength of commitment to equality for women' (*The Times*, 1985).

The debate over the taxation of married couples was resolved in the Budget of 1988. This introduced independent taxation of husband and wife, to take effect in 1990. The changes meant that each partner had his or her own tax allowance which was not transferable to the other partner. The married man's tax allowance remained, in the form of a 'married couple's allowance' to be set against the husband's earnings but transferred to the wife if he did not have enough income to be liable for tax. The continuation of a special higher allowance for married couples represented ideological support for the institution of marriage; paying the allowance to married men seemed to represent an affirmation of male dominance within marriage.

However, the move to independent taxation represented a fundamental ideological shift. Instead of treating husband and wife as a unit, they were henceforth to be regarded as two separate individuals, at least in the eyes of the Inland Revenue. Instead of being incorporated into the person of their husbands, at least as far as taxation was concerned, the changes meant that wives could have privacy and independence in managing their financial affairs. It will be interesting to see whether the ideological shift will be followed by a decrease in the proportion of couples who pool their incomes and share the management of their money.

The 1988 changes in taxation did nothing to help parents with the costs of child care. The decision to opt for non-transferable allowances gave no financial assistance to couples where one partner was unable to earn because of responsibility for young children. One form of assistance would have been to make the costs of child care tax deductable, either for individual parents or for employers. This would have represented recognition of the cost of child rearing and support for the employment of parents. Another form of financial assistance would have been an increase in child benefit. A leader writer in the *Financial Times* argued that husband and wife should have equal, but non-transferable allowances, while the costs of child care should be met through the social security system: 'the introduction of non-transferable allowances could be accompanied by 2 pence off the basic rate (of tax), a rise in child benefit to £12, and substantial increases in supplementary benefit and unemployment benefits. Non-transferable allowances would free resources to help the really disadvantaged' (*Financial Times*, 1988).

Conclusion

Current arrangements reflect conflicting ideologies. Thus the married couple's tax allowance is the product of patriarchal ideologies which define the man as the head of the household and the breadwinner. It is an allowance which benefits earners over non-earners and tax payers over non-tax payers: that is, it benefits richer and employed men as opposed to poorer men, unemployed men and all women. The married couple's tax allowance presupposes that the man will share his additional income with other members of the household; the payment of child benefit to mothers reflects the recognition that in reality some men do not do this.

In all these debates it is rarely suggested that a mother of young children might be entitled to an income in her own right. When she is caring for a dependent child she can claim 'child benefit' not 'mother's benefit', which makes it clear that though she is responsible for the money it is not intended that she should spend it on herself. People bringing up children on a low income can claim 'family credit', not 'mother's credit', even though the benefit typically replaces the mother's earnings in the family budget. The additional income received by a husband whose tax allowance reflects his responsibility for a dependent wife is unequivocally his and not hers. When a self-employed husband claims to employ his wife as a secretary or book-keeper in order to gain the advantage of her tax allowance as well as his, there is no guarantee that she will get the money which he claims he has paid her: some wives do not even know that their husbands are receiving additional untaxed income which represents the work done by the wife. All these examples underline the point that, though the tax and benefit systems recognise the costs of the work for which women are responsible, it reimburses those costs, not to women themselves and in their own right, but to husbands, or to mothers as trustees for their children. For women, caring is still a labour of love and the price of caring continues to be their own economic dependency (Finch and Groves, 1983).

In making changes the tax and benefit systems must be considered together. The change to independent taxation benefitted two earner households as opposed to those with one earner or no earners. If it is not to exacerbate inequality it should be linked to a substantial increase in child benefit or to some other compensation to those who are not earning, or who cannot earn because of their responsibility for dependants. In making proposals for change it is important to recognise the different structural positions of men and women, and of earners and non-earners, and to compensate for, rather than exacerbate the inequalities which already exist.

The research described in this book has produced new evidence for the debate. As we saw in chapter 7, an increase in women's earnings produced a bigger proportional rise in the amount spent on housekeeping than an equivalent rise in men's earnings. Giving additional money to mothers, whether in the form of wages or social security payments, is likely to produce bigger increases in the living standards of children than giving the same sum of money to fathers.

9

Money and power in marriage

The aim in this chapter will be to draw together the conclusions of the study and to set them in a broader context. The study has shown that, though financial arrangements within marriage may take an economic form, their significance cannot be understood without taking account of social structures, processes and meanings. The financial arrangements of married couples reflect not only practical convenience and individual choice, but also the social and economic circumstances of people's lives and their ideas about the nature of marriage. Patterns of allocation of money change over time, as chapters 2 and 3 showed: this is a very complex process which reflects changes in economic conditions, in employment patterns, in legislation, in social relationships and in ideologies.

Earning and spending may mark the points at which money enters and leaves the intra-household economy, but that economy is far more complex than the 'black box' model of the household would suggest. Who spends the money and what they buy with it reflect, not only the crude level of household income, but also who earned the money, who has overall control and who manages it on a day-to-day basis. Where household income is low the finances are likely to be controlled and managed by the wife. At higher income levels the husband is likely to control finances, especially if he is the only earner, though he will usually delegate management of part of the household income to his wife. Where both partners earn, management is likely to be shared, though overall control may still reflect the relative earning power and the economic contribution of each of the two individuals involved. Compared with 30 years ago, more couples now share the management of household income; however, there are still many marriages where husbands control and manage finances and where wives' access to money is severely limited.

The amount spent on housekeeping, that is on food and daily living expenses, reflects the control of money in the household and the economic contribution of each partner. Where a wife controls the money a household is likely to spend a higher proportion of its income on housekeeping; money earned by wives is more likely to be spent on food and daily living expenses than is money earned by husbands. Thus household financial arrangements can be seen as occupying a crucial intersection, between the economic and the social, between the economy outside the household and that within it. As Fitz and Hood-Williams pointed out, in the midst of capitalism we have an entrenched system of distribution which is not capitalist, but upon which capitalism relies (1982, p. 66).

The study provided an opportunity to compare husbands' and wives' answers to the same questions and to explore the differences between 'his' marriage and 'her' marriage. Husbands typically earned more than wives and had more fringe benefits from their employment. They usually saw themselves as breadwinners for the family, even when they retained substantial sums for their own use; wives' earnings were seen as more marginal to the budget, even though most women spent their wages on the family. Husbands were less likely to have to justify the money they spent and they tended to spend more on their own leisure. In general, husbands were likely to perceive a greater degree of sharing in marriage than wives, who were more aware of conflicts of opinion and of interest.

Many couples wanted their marriage to be a relationship between equals and tried to express this equality in their financial arrangements. However, the results of the study showed that the greater earning power of husbands continues to be associated with greater control over finances and greater power in decision making within the family. When a wife becomes the chief earner this challenges traditional ideologies: the discomfort which such a situation provokes is evidence of the continuing power of ideology. Patriarchal ideologies have the effect of legitimating the power of husbands, even when couples express a desire for greater equality, and constraining the power of wives, even if they earn more than their partners.

These results illuminate the complex nature of the conjugal contract. The term implies an equal and agreed bargain between husband and wife, in which financial support is exchanged for domestic work and child care. Yet the contract is not between equals, since few women earn enough to support a husband and children and fewer men would agree to accept the loss of life time earnings experienced by most wives and mothers (Joshi, 1987). Inequality in the wider society meshes with inequality within the household. A woman may contribute a higher proportion of her earnings to housekeeping than her husband, but her income is still likely to be regarded as marginal; a man may contribute a lower proportion of his earnings but he still feels justified in spending more than his wife on leisure because both define him as the breadwinner.

The relationship between the state and marriage in this context is extremely complex. There has been little legislation specifically concerned with the allocation of money within marriage: this is usually explained by reference to the private nature of marriage and the inappropriateness of outside interference. However, this has not prevented the passing of legislation which reflects assumptions about how couples allocate their money. Indeed it is impossible to avoid the issue since, for example, couples either have to be taxed as one unit or as two individuals and income maintenance payments cannot be made both on a household and on an individual basis.

The new community charge, or poll tax, which has replaced local rates in Britain, illustrates this dilemma. The White Paper which heralded the new tax commented that 'in principle each individual should be individually liable for paying his or her bill', but recognised that this might not be practicable where a person had no independent income. The solution which was adopted was to make husbands and wives jointly and severally liable for each other's community charges. The paragraph concluded: 'This would reflect the practical financial arrangements which most married couples with only one earner adopt. It would also reflect the arrangements which the social security system makes by assessing married couples jointly' (Secretary of State for the Environment, 1986, p. 111).

The process of economic development provides many examples, drawn from many different parts of the world, of the dangers of ignoring the intra-household economy. In a review of the growing literature on this topic Blumberg concludes that the recent famines in Africa occurred partly because development planners have neglected to take account of financial arrangements within families. She argues that over much of the continent women raise the bulk of locally consumed food crops, but that they rarely benefit from agricultural development projects. In many parts of Africa husband and wife maintain separate purses and separate obligations for spending. If a development project fails to provide economic returns to women both the project and the standard of living of women and children, are likely to suffer. Blumberg concludes that the combination of a gender-differentiated household economy, female predominance in food crops grown for local consumption, and insufficient incentives to women producers may be an important but unrecognised factor in Africa's recent food crises (Blumberg, 1988; see also Carloni, 1987).

Development planners have tended to direct resources to the household as a unit, or to the nominal household head, while ignoring the very different spending patterns of women and men. There are now a number of detailed empirical studies of this issue which have been drawn together by Dwyer and Bruce (1988). Their conclusion is very important. Though in absolute terms men may contribute more to the household economy than do women, in relative terms women typically contribute a higher proportion of their income to the household's basic needs, and especially to the needs of children. Compared with men, women hold less back, both absolutely and relatively, for their personal use. Since the goal of many development planners is to raise the standard of living of children it follows that the best way to do this is to direct economic aid to women.

It is interesting that the research described in this book produced a similar result: though husbands typically contributed more absolutely to housekeeping, wives typically contributed a larger proportion of their income. The implications for policy are also similar. The best way to raise the living standard of poor children is to increase the amount of money over which their mothers have control. This would also have the effect of increasing the power of women within the family, as the following analysis shows.

Power and decision-making

There is an enormous literature on power in marriage and on the difficulty of defining exactly what the concept means in this context. There is not space to discuss this literature here, nor is there any need since there have been several comprehensive surveys of the field (Safilios Rothschild, 1970; Cromwell and Olson, 1975; Scanzoni, 1979; McDonald, 1980). In attempting to measure power empirically most researchers have used information about which partner makes specific decisions. This approach has been criticised for giving the same weight to decisions of different importance, for neglecting the processes which precede making a decision, and for ignoring the structural inequalities between men and women (Gillespie, 1971; Edgell, 1980). Nevertheless the great majority of those who have investigated the determinants of power in marriage have used the making of decisions as a measure; my study followed in that tradition, inadequate though it may be as a way of assessing so elusive a concept as power.

In the study we ended each interview by listing various decisions and asking whether each was likely to be made by the husband alone, the husband in consultation with his wife, both partners together, the wife in consultation with her husband, or the wife alone. The decisions which were presented were: organising finances; buying a car; buying a consumer good such as a washing machine; what to do at Christmas; where to go on holiday; deciding something to do with the husband's job; deciding something to do with the wife's job. Given five possible answers to each of seven different decisions it was possible to create a score which ran in theory from seven, if a husband decided everything alone, to 35 if a wife decided everything alone. A score of 21 implied equality between husband and wife in decision-making and occurred either because all the answers were 'we decide together' or because the husband's greater power in one decision was balanced by the wife's in another. A score of over 21 meant that the wife played a dominant role in decision-making, while a score of less than 21 meant that the husband was dominant. The separate interviews meant that there was one decision-making score for the wife and another for the husband.

It was interesting to see that the husbands' answers to this question did not correlate closely with the wives'. Only 48 out of the 102 couples agreed about which partner was dominant in decision-making. This result, which has been observed by other researchers, underlines the danger of studying marriage through the eyes of one partner; it is also a reminder of the differences between 'her' marriage and 'his' marriage. In the analysis which follows the answers given by husband and wife have been combined to produce a joint decision-making score.

The analysis provided confirmation that the questions about decision-making did indeed measure something which might be described as power. There were statistically significant correlations between the three power scores and two other key measures of power in marriage. These were, first, the interviewers' assessment of which partner spoke most authoritatively in the joint interview and, secondly, the wives' answers to the question, 'Who really controls the money in this household?'.

Table 9.1 shows that where the husband played a major role in decision-making, his wife was likely to identify him as controlling the money; conversely, when a wife played a major role in decision-making she was likely to feel that she controlled the money. It was interesting to see that the husband's assessment of who controlled the money correlated poorly with decision making. Perhaps husbands took the business of being interviewed less seriously, or perhaps they were simply less aware of the realities of power in marriage? At all events this finding provides support for the decision to use the wife's assessment of who controls the money in constructing the typology of control of finances, developed at the end of chapter 5 and used for the analysis in chapters 6 and 7.

Husbands were more likely to be dominant in decision-making than were wives. This was so whether the answers used were those of the wife or of the husband. In about half of the couples the husband was defined as dominant, while the rest of the sample were divided

Table 9.1 *Control of money by dominance in decision making*

Wife sees money as controlled by	Dominant partner in decision making		
	Husband	Both equally	Wife
Husband	25	9	3
Both equally	8	14	2
Wife	12	15	14
Total number	45	38	19

between equality and wife-dominance in decision-making. Combining the answers given by husband and wife produced a larger number of couples who appeared to be equal in decision-making, but husbands still dominated.

Previous research on decision-making in marriage has suggested that the partner with the larger income is likely to play a more dominant part in decision-making and that wives are likely to have greater decision-making power if they are in paid employment rather than working at home; older wives are likely to be more dominant in decision-making, partly because they are more likely to be in paid work. This study offered an opportunity to explore the economic inequality between husbands and wives, not just in terms of how much each partner earned, but also in terms of who controlled and managed money within the household.

Money may confer power outside the household: is the same true inside the household? What happens to the link between money and power as money passes from earners to spenders? Does power in decision-making remain with the partner who earns the money or does it pass to the partner who controls or manages finances?

The results confirmed the link between inequality outside the household and inequality in decision-making within the household. Husbands were more likely to dominate decision-making where the wife did not have a job, as Table 9.2 shows; conversely wives who were dominant in decision-making were usually in paid employment. Other analyses, not presented here, showed that younger women and those with small children were less likely to dominate in decision-making than older women. It was interesting to see that some couples had a much greater degree of equality in decision-making, while others were polarised between husband and wife dominance. Equality seemed to be associated with couples being in their thirties, with having the house in their joint names as opposed to in his name alone, and with both partners having stayed on at school after the leaving age and having acquired post-school qualifications.

Though Table 9.2 is interesting it is not statistically significant according to conventional tests; on the other hand Table 9.3 is highly significant ($p < 0.01$). Until this point in the argument it has not seemed appropriate to lay great stress on tests of significance because of the small numbers involved. However, the contrast between these two tables is important. It seems as if power, as

Table 9.2 *Employment pattern by dominance in decision making*

	Dominant partner in decision making		
Employment	Husband	Both equally	Wife
Both employed	17	19	14
Wife only	–	1	–
Husband only	22	15	3
Neither employed	6	3	2
Total number	45	38	19

measured by dominance in decision-making, was associated more strongly with the control of finances *within* the household than it was with factors external to the house, such as income or employment pattern.

Table 9.3 shows that where wives had power in terms of decision-making it was likely that the couple would operate the system which I have called wife-controlled pooling; this means that the couple had a joint account and that the wife controlled the couple's finances. Where the husband dominated decision-making it was likely that financial arrangements would be either husband-controlled pooling or husband control, that is, the husband controlled finances, whether or not the couple had a joint account. Equality in decision-making was associated with having a joint account. Taken together

Table 9.3 *Control of finances by dominance in decision making*

	Dominant partner in decision making		
Control of finances	Husband	Both equally	Wife
Wife control	6	5	3
Wife-controlled pooling	6	10	11
Husband-controlled pooling	21	16	2
Husband control	12	7	3
Total number	45	38	19

Tables 9.2 and 9.3 suggest that very poor couples, where neither partner is in employment, are associated with quite high levels of husband-dominance; the fact that wives controlled finances in these households was not necessarily associated with the wife being dominant in decision-making.

Analysing power in decision-making according to the couple's system of money management produced comparable results. The allowance system and the independent management system were associated with decision-making dominance by the husband, while shared management of money was associated with equality in decision-making. However, these associations were only marginally significant. The strongest association, therefore, was that between power in decision-making and the control of finances. One can conclude that the link between money and power holds inside the household as well as outside it; however, power in decision-making is more strongly associated with controlling money than with managing it.

Finally, there is the question which all researchers on this topic are asked sooner or later: 'Which is the best way of organising money in marriage?' 'Best' may be defined in terms of convenience, in terms of never getting into financial difficulties, or in terms of acceptability to one or both partners. However, many people are interested in knowing whether there is any association between happiness and specific financial arrangements. Questions about happiness in marriage are notoriously prone to bias: few people are willing to admit that their marriage is unsatisfactory, at least in response to a single question in a single interview. So in the interviews moderately unhappy people tended to say their marriage was 'average', and

Table 9.4   *Marital happiness by control of finances*
Wives' answers (husbands' answers in brackets)

Marriage described as	Wife control	Wife-controlled pooling	Husband-controlled pooling	Husband control
Happy/very happy	13 (13)	23 (25)	37 (35)	13 (16)
Average/unhappy	1 (1)	4 (2)	2 (4)	9 (6)
Total number	14	27	39	22

anyone who admitted to problems was likely to be quite unhappy; the answers on this topic were corroborated by the interviewers, who had watched the interaction between the couple in the joint interview.

Respondents were asked 'Would you say that your marriage is very happy, happy, average, unhappy or very unhappy?' Those who described themselves as 'average' were grouped with those who were unhappy. Table 9.4 shows the results. In the sample as a whole only one-sixth of couples felt that their marriage was unhappy, but where husbands controlled the money this proportion rose to a quarter of the men and nearly two-fifths of the women. We cannot be certain whether husband-control leads to unhappiness or whether marital discord provokes the husband into taking control of finances. However, there was a very significant association between male control of money and marital unhappiness and this applied equally to men and to women.

Future directions

Since I began work on this topic there has been a surge of interest in financial arrangements within households. In the final pages I consider what has been achieved and what remains to be done. My own research has been used as evidence in a number of different debates. Government departments which have expressed an interest in it include the Inland Revenue, the Law Commission, the Department of Employment, the Department of Health and Social Security and the Office of Population Censuses and Surveys; it has been used by the Equal Opportunities Commission, the Child Poverty Action Group and the Family Policy Studies Centre (Platt, 1987). That so much interest should be shown in a relatively small scale study underlines the importance of the topic and the need for further, and better, research.

One problem is that until now most of the studies which have investigated the distribution of resources within households have collected information from relatively small numbers of people, while large-scale surveys of standards of living have tended to take the household as the unit of analysis (compare Brannen and Wilson, 1987, with Walker and Parker, 1987). In Britain there are a number of long-running national surveys which are potential sources of information. The Family Expenditure Survey and the General Household Survey both collect information from individuals but present it in terms of households. It would be valuable if official surveys such as these could begin to include questions on intra-household economic activity. At the same time it would be valuable to have a large scale survey specifically about the allocation of money within the household. This would make it possible to find out to what extent patterns of allocation of money vary between different geographical locations and between different occupational and cultural groups. It might also make it possible to discover more about the financial arrangements of the very rich, a group who were conspicuously missing from my study.

Recent work on the allocation of money within households has also made a contribution to the literature on poverty. It has become clear that, far from protecting them, women's assumed and actual dependence on men constitutes a major cause of their poverty (Glendinning and Millar, 1987, p. 26). Women carry the burden of scarcity, not just because they are more likely than men to be poor, but also because when a household is poor it is women who are usually responsible for seeing that the money goes round; when money is short it is typically women who go without. The recent idea of the 'feminisation of poverty' implies that women are now at greater risk of poverty than men (Scott, 1984). However, evidence from Britain suggests that throughout the twentieth century women have been more likely to fall into poverty than men (Lewis and Piachaud, 1987). It is simply that in recent years women's poverty, and their responsibility for managing scarce resources, have been better documented (Ashley, 1983; Wilson, 1987).

Money is not the only resource which is exchanged within households. One achievement of the last few years has been an increase in our knowledge about the distribution of a variety of different resources. These may take the form of material resources such as time and space, or human resources such as skill, knowledge and energy (Brannen and Wilson, 1987). An individual's right to a particular resource may depend, for example, on gender, on age, or on the amount of money which he or she contributes to the household. Thus in large families time and space tend to be scarce resources and women are more likely than men to bear the brunt of shortages in either (Land, 1969). High status foods are consumed more often by adults than by children, and more often by men than women (Charles and Kerr, 1988; Kerr and Charles, 1986; Delphy,

1984; Murcott, 1982). Women are more likely than men to have to care for others, while men are more likely to be cared for, or at least to be released from the responsibility to care (Baldwin, 1985; Finch and Groves, 1983; Ungerson, 1987). Young adults of all social classes are likely to receive financial subsidies from parents when they marry and set up house (Leonard, 1980). However, as people grow older the resources which they give and receive change: elderly middle class people are likely to be providing financial help to the next generation, while elderly working class people are more likely to be receiving goods and domestic help from their children (Qureshi and Simons, 1987). It would be interesting to have more research on the control and allocation of different sorts of resources within households and on their interchangeability.

It would also be useful to know more about the allocation of money within other relationships than marriage and within other sorts of households. To what extent do adult brothers and sisters give each other financial help? What happens to the allocation of money within the household when the parents are unemployed and the chief earner is the teenage son or daughter? Do different ethnic groups have different norms about family finances? What could a longitudinal study of money management tell us about the processes of household formation and dissolution? When divorce and re-marriage produce complex families, within which a child may have four 'parents' and eight 'grandparents', what is the effect on financial arrangements? And what happens to the allocation of money within the growing number of households which give 'care in the community' to people leaving mental handicap and mental illness hospitals? Answers to questions such as these would help to inform a range of policy decisions, as well as enhancing our understanding of contemporary society.

Money offers a means of exploring both the relationships between individuals within households and also the links between households and the wider society. Money functions as a signifier, or indicator, which makes it possible to trace the effects of social and economic processes. Flows of money within households provide a means of examining the significance of gender, age and life cycle stage. The tension between the economic and the social, between ideology and practice, between the individual and the couple, between earning and spending, can all be explored through investigating the control and allocation of money within marriage.

Appendix 1

Researching money and marriage

A variety of different methods could have been employed to explore the ways in which couples organise their money. At one extreme the study could have taken the form of a large scale questionnaire survey, carried out in different parts of Britain in order to investigate regional variations, with enough interviews to allow for sophisticated statistical analysis. This strategy, however, seemed neither appropriate nor practical. A questionnaire survey risks losing the rich complexity of ordinary life in the search for a data set which collects similar information from each respondent in a form which can be readily coded and analysed: complicated issues such as the distribution of power within marriage are not easily investigated by means of structured questionnaires. In addition, large numbers of interviews require a team of interviewers and, however skilled and sensitive they may be, this sets up yet another barrier between the reality of human experience and its translation into a written account. Above all, however, a large scale survey was made impossible by the expense and time involved.

On the other hand, the study could have been more qualitative and ethnographic in style. This might have involved a series of interviews with different members of small number of families, set in the context of continuing contacts between the researcher and the families. The aim here would have been to build up a detailed knowledge, not just of how money was controlled and allocated, but also of the meaning money had for individual family members. A qualitative approach has many advantages in tackling a problematic and sensitive subject such as this. For example, the researcher faces the problem of reconciling the discrepancies between the differing accounts of different actors. There may be discrepancies between, first, what a couple actually do with their money, secondly, what they think they do, thirdly, what they are prepared to admit to an interviewer and fourthly, what the interviewer perceives as important enough to write down; there are likely to be further discrepancies between the accounts which husband and wife give of the same financial event, accounts which are likely to consist of a mix of facts, expressions of opinion, implicit and explicit value judgements, and so on. In coping with all this a qualitative approach has great advantages over more quantitative methods. Again, however, constraints of time and cost are relevant. If the study is not to take an inordinate length of time, the number of families would have to be severely limited, with the result that it would become impossible to carry out any statistical analyses and difficult to generalise from these few families to a wider population.

Faced with these dilemmas I adopted a strategy which attempted to combine the advantages of both quantitative and qualitative methods: inevitably, of course, this produced a mix of the disadvantages of both. The completed study eventually involved interviews with 102 married couples, each with at least one child under 16. Though my original interest had been in the more general issue of how money is controlled and allocated within families, I decided to limit the number of variables to be explored by focusing on married, or as-married couples, controlling for stage in the family life cycle by selecting couples with at least one dependent child. I was also forced to neglect regional variations as an independent variable because shortage of resources compelled me to do all the interviews in Kent. I attempted to compensate for this by making as much use as I could of comparable studies, carried out in other parts of Britain or other countries.

Having decided that I was interested in financial arrangements among couples with dependent children, I was faced with the problem of finding a population with these characteristics and selecting a sample of it. Random door knocking and direct approaches to people listed in the electoral register seemed likely to provoke resistance when the interviews might so easily be confused with those carried out by market research firms. Given the sensitivity of the topic and the demanding nature of the interviews I felt that potential respondents should receive warning in the form of a letter, though I was aware that this might reduce the response rate. Age-sex registers held by health centres seemed to offer access to a nearly-complete population of families, since the great majority of children are registered with a general practitioner. Recent research has suggested that in a well kept age-sex register under-registration is less of a problem than over-registration, which in one study accounted for 8 per cent of those on the register at any one time (Cobb and Miles, 1983). Understandably, many health centres are reluctant to allow researchers whose work is not immediately relevant to health care to have access to their age-sex registers. I am grateful to those who made me welcome.

The three health centres through which respondents were contacted were located in three rather different places. The first was a large mining village, built in the early years of the twentieth century when the Kent coal field was first developed. The patients registered at the health centre came from an isolated rural area and of the families whom we interviewed nearly a third were directly dependent on the coal mine. The second health centre faced the sea, in a fishing and holiday town with a population of 30,000 in 1981. Finally, the third centre was located in a small country town of 16,000 people, with a picturesque historic centre and some industry. Approximately one third of the sample came from each of these places; however, differences between the three were not significant so the sample has been treated as one throughout the study.

The interviews

Each couple was interviewed first together and then separately, at the same time but in different rooms. This strategy was a response to methodological problems thrown up by previous research. Many studies of marriage and family life are based on interviews with one spouse or one family member, usually the wife since she is more likely to be at home and more amenable to being interviewed. The predominance of this approach has given rise to the criticism that family sociology would be better described as 'wives' family sociology (Safilios-Rothschild, 1969). I wanted to be sure that the differences between 'his' marriage and 'her' marriage would be properly expressed in the data.

Another problem specifically affects studies of money. There is now a considerable body of knowledge to suggest that wives, in particular, may not be aware of how much their husbands earn or may underestimate those earnings. (See, for example, Gorer, 1971; Marsh 1978, p. 13.) Since it was likely that levels of wifely ignorance would vary, and that husbands too might be ignorant of their wives' financial position, it seemed important to get individual answers from each spouse.

Interviewing husband and wife first together and then separately caused problems of at least three different sorts. First, this method undoubtedly contributed to the low response rate. Of the couples who were approached, only 52 per cent agreed to be interviewed. The low response rate seemed to reflect partly the fact that money was defined as too private a topic for discussion with a stranger, and partly the fact that both wife and husband were to be interviewed. Many individuals who were willing to participate did not do so because their spouses were reluctant or unwilling. Men were more likely to refuse than women. The attitude of many refusing couples was summed up by one woman who said, 'I wouldn't mind myself. But my husband doesn't want to do it because he says "What's our business is our business" '.

Secondly, the method gave rise to practical problems. Clearly it was impossible for me to do all the interviews, both because of the number to be completed and because of the separate but concurrent interviews. Seven interviewers helped with the project, after a special training to familiarise them with its aims and methods. Carrying out the interviews took ten months, much longer than had been anticipated. This was largely because each separate interview required the presence of four people, the two respondents and two interviewers, and so there were often long delays between contacting a couple and completing an interview with them. However, the practical problems were amply justified by the results. There were frequently wide discrepancies between the husband's answers and the wife's answers to the same question, as we have seen. The results showed that studies which use either husband or wife as respondent on behalf of the couple cannot make the assumption that the answers represent the position of the partner who was not interviewed.

These responses gave rise to a third set of problems, to do with interpretation. Since the questionnaires for the separate interviews of wife and husband were almost identical, the answers to some questions could take the form of 'her answer', 'his answer' and 'the difference between the two answers'. These discrepancies are open to various different interpretations. They might reflect the fact that each spouse had different knowledge on a given issue; they might reflect similar knowledge, differently perceived; or the discrepancy might be the result of a careless answer, a deliberate desire to deceive or an interviewer who misinterpreted what was said. All these possibilities occurred at one time or another; the problem in interpreting the results was to distinguish between different causes of discrepancy.

Once a couple had agreed to be interviewed the interview itself was usually easier than might have been expected. The joint interview normally took place in the living room, with one interviewer sitting quietly while the other asked the questions. Going on to the separate interviews gave rise to a variety of responses from complete acceptance to wry amusement, and it usually took the form of one spouse and interviewer moving into the kitchen. As the study progressed the interviewers developed the hypothesis that the partner who controlled the money remained in the living room, but unfortunately this idea came too late to be investigated systematically!

The questionnaire

The questionnaire was designed not only to explore the hypotheses outlined at the beginning of Chapter 4 but also to minimise the effects of some of the problems the study posed. The pilot interviews were tape recorded, but in the main study the interviewers simply noted answers to questions, writing down verbatim comments from respondents if these seemed illuminating. In research of this sort there is always a problem about choosing at what stage in the research process to sift and reduce the messy complexity of reality to the relative simplicity needed for a coherent account. The use of a pre-coded, highly structured questionnaire means that most of the sifting has already been done before the interview begins, leaving the respondent, as it were, to fill in the boxes already created by the research. On the other hand, unstructured, tape-recorded interviews give the respondent an opportunity to initiate new lines of enquiry and to challenge the researcher's definition of the situation. The advantages of less structured interviews are particularly great when the study focuses on people who lack power and whose point of view may have been over-ridden by more dominant individuals and groups. For this reason this approach to data collection has been favoured by feminists seeking to understand the experience of different sorts of women in a male-dominated world (Bell and Roberts, 1984; Roberts, 1981).

The problem with unstructured, tape-recorded interviews is that they produce a mass of material which has to be codified at a later stage in the research process, an exercise which can be both difficult and time consuming. For this reason I adopted the compromise solution of a structured questionnaire, with verbatim comments noted down at the time and with only a small number of tape-recorded interviews. In designing the questionnaire I drew on that used in the study carried out by Edwards (1981).

A number of other strategies supplemented the data from the formal interviews. For example, at the end of each joint interview, the interviewers systematically noted down which partner had talked most and which had seemed most authoritative on the subject of money. This was because the idea of power in marriage is notoriously difficult to measure empirically. The questionnaire itself contained scales designed to measure marital power, as well as direct questions to the spouses, both together and separately, about which one of them had greater control of money. However, it seemed important to approach the issue of power from as many different directions as possible: observation of how the couple dealt with a joint interview offered another method of assessing whether one partner deferred to the other over money matters.

In addition, the two interviewers, after they had left the house, noted down their own subjective comments on the couple, their response to the interview and their account of how they organised their money. It might be argued that this was second-hand data, being the interviewers' perception of how couples organised their money rather than from a direct account by the couple themselves. However, having two interviewers meant that the two accounts could be compared and the understanding gained from these often helped to illuminate the factual answers written on the questionnaires.

The joint interviews collected information about the household as a whole and the couple as a unit. Questions were asked about all members of the household and their employment, if any. Using a check list of items on which the family might have to spend money, the couple were asked who actually paid for each item. A series of open-ended questions was concerned with how money was organised within the household, and more general questions explored subjective evaluation of standards of living and attitudes to money.

The separate interviews investigated these and other issues, but from the points of view of the individual spouses. The questionnaires were almost identical for husband and wife. Having asked about parents and how they organised their money, the interview collected background information about each individual's education, employment and marriage. Detailed questions about income from all possible sources, and savings, were followed by questions about the income of other members of the family. A section about current and savings accounts in banks and building societies provided additional insights into how money was controlled and allocated. The next set of questions explored housekeeping money, personal spending money and expenditure on leisure. The following section, which turned out to be of central importance, was concerned with why the couple organised their finances as they did and how each partner felt about their financial arrangements. Consumption patterns and standard of living were investigated in a series of questions about spending on food and housing, hire-purchase, debt, credit and credit cards, the ownership of consumer durables and each individual's experience of material hardship. Other questions explored attitudes to social security and especially to child benefit. The interview concluded with a section about decision-making within marriage.

When a research project has been completed it is tantalising to consider how, in retrospect, things should have been done. However, for the benefit of those who may investigate the issue in the future it might be useful to consider alternative possibilities. In many ways the study described here was a compromise. Thus the questionnaire was both too structured and also not detailed enough. It was too tightly structured in that it did not allow couples to describe their financial arrangements in their own way and following their own logic. Some of the questions, on some occasions, met with bewilderment, amusement or rejection. For example, the same questions about housekeeping money were asked of wives for whom getting more housekeeping money involved a bitter argument with their husbands as well as of wives who, if they needed more money, simply took more out of the common pool. The latter group were puzzled to be asked 'How do you go about getting an increase in housekeeping money?' or 'What do you do if you run out of money?' A slightly different problem, but one with the same basic cause, appeared in the answers to the question 'If you won or inherited £5000 what would you do with the money?'. Some people found it hard to contemplate spending so large a sum, while one man commented 'Five thousand pounds, not much really'.

The same questions were asked of all respondents in order to get comparable data for all, but it is important to remember that the significance of the answers they gave, and the contexts in which they answered were not comparable. An alternative research strategy, drawing on anthropological techniques, might have been more appropriate. In such a study questionnaires could be abandoned in favour of checklists of topics to be covered, and the researcher would spend time getting to know each respondent reasonably well in order to gain a better understanding of the ways in which financial arrangements reflected other aspects of the life of the individual, the couple and the household.

Alternatively, the data collection instruments could have been more detailed. In particular they could have included detailed diaries of expenditure, following the technique used, for example by the Family Expenditure Survey (Office of Population Censuses and Surveys, 1985). Here each adult member of the household is asked to keep a detailed diary of daily spending for a fortnight. If the diaries had documented not only spending but also details of income and of transfers within the household, they could have provided a valuable additional source of data, as well as a check on answers to the more subjective questions. This method was used by MacLeod in his study in Newcastle and provided valuable evidence about the relationships between total household income and the amounts spent by individuals on particular items. However, the prospect of having to complete a budget deterred some families from taking part in that study, and among those who did take part only 59 per cent filled in the budget records (MacLeod, 1977). Anticipating these difficulties and the problems involved in analysing such an enormous quantity of data, I decided not to collect detailed information on spending.

The section of the questionnaire which dealt with income followed the Family Expenditure Survey in focusing on the previous pay period; self-employed people were offered three different ways of calculating their incomes and their answers were converted to weekly or yearly averages for the analysis (Kemsley *et al.*, 1980). All income data presented in the text represents take-home pay.

The couples who took part in the study

A total of 102 married couples, all living within 30 miles of each other, cannot be said to be representative of any larger population. Yet inevitably there is the temptation to generalise from the results of this study. So it is relevant to consider whether the people who took part in the study were similar to, or different from larger populations which they might be said to represent. Tables A1.1 to A1.6 make such comparisons, in terms of a number of different characteristics. The couples who took part in the study are compared with the British population as a whole, or where possible with sub-sections of the population, such as married couples of comparable ages; the data are taken from years as close as possible to those when the interviews took place.

The tables show that in many respects the study couples were not as a group substantially different from a much wider population. Table A1.1 gives information about employment, using national data collected for the General Household Survey in 1983. It shows that while in Britain as a whole 48 per cent of married women with dependent children were in employment in 1983, in the study sample the proportion was 50 per cent. At a time when

Table A1.1　*Patterns of employment*

	This study N = 102 %	Married couples with dependent children Britain 1983* %
Husband and wife both employed	49	45
Husband not employed, wife employed	1	3
Husband employed, wife not employed	39	43
Neither partner employed	11	10

* Office of Population Censuses and Surveys, 1985

for 10 per cent of British couples neither partner was in employment, the proportion among the couples who took part in the study was 11 per cent.

Table A1.2 makes comparisons in terms of social class and again there are reassuring similarities. However, the sample did differ in small but important respects from the British population as a whole. Class is defined in the table according to the Registrar General's classification of occupations. The figures show that among the couples who took part in the study there were smaller proportions of people from both the higher and lower ends of the social scale, so that both professionals and unskilled manual workers were under-represented.

The point of using social class is, of course, to predict from this one dimension of a person's life whether he or she is likely to be more or less advantaged along other dimensions. Housing tenure is sometimes used in a similar way. Table A1.3 shows that in this respect the couples in the sample were remarkably similar to couples in England as a whole In both groups nearly three-quarters of all households owned their own homes, while just over one-quarter rented from a local authority or from a private landlord. In Table A1.3 comparisons are made between the sample couples and married male heads of households aged between 30 and 44. This categorisation was chosen in order to be able to make comparisons between groups of married couples, since single people and single parent households do have rather different patterns of housing tenure. The age range was chosen because the great majority of those who took part in the study were aged between 30 and 44: 19 per cent of wives were under 30, 70 per cent between

Table A1.2 *Social class*

	Women		Men	
	This study %	Britain 1983* %	This study %	Britain 1983* %
Professional	–	1	3	6
Intermediate	18	21	40	24
Skilled non-manual	35	35	4	8
Skilled manual	12	8	40	40
Semi-skilled manual	28	28	13	17
Unskilled manual	6	8	–	5

* Office of Population Censuses and Surveys, 1985

Note: The figures for Britain refer to women aged 16–59 and men aged 16–64; class is based on current or most recent occupation.

Table A1.3   *Housing tenure*

	This study	Married male heads of households in England: 1981	
		aged 30–34	aged 35–44*
	%	%	%
Owner occupier	72	70	73
Tenant	28	30	27

* Department of the Environment, 1981

30 and 44, and 12 per cent over 45, while the comparable figures for husbands were 7 per cent, 78 per cent and 15 per cent.

What sorts of families took part in the study? Out of the 102 couples, 101 were legally married, while one couple were living together in a stable relationship with their two children. However, all were described as married couples for the sake of convenience. For most individuals this was their first marriage, but 11 per cent of the women and 9 per cent of the husbands had been married before. All the couples had at least one dependent child, since this was one criterion for inclusion in the study. However, as Table A1.4 shows, by comparison with the general population of married couples in Britain, fewer of the study couples had only one child and more had three or more children. There is no obvious explanation for the larger family size of the couples in the study.

Tables A1.5 and A1.6 are concerned with different ways of assessing standard of living. In terms of the ownership of consumer durables the couples in the study were very similar to the total population of households

Table A1.4   *Numbers of dependent children*

	This study	Married couples with dependent children in Britain, 1983*
	%	%
One child	17	38
Two children	49	43
Three children	24	15
Four or more children	11	4

* Office of Population Censuses and Surveys, 1985

Table A1.5 *Ownership of consumer durables*

	This study %	Families in Britain 1983* %
Colour television	86	87
Video recorder	23	27
Fridge	100	97
Washing machine	99	95
Dishwasher	7	7
Telephone	82	80
Car	75	60

* Office of Population Censuses and Surveys, 1985

with children in Britain. All the couples in the sample owned a fridge and 99 per cent a washing machine; 86 per cent had a colour television and 82 per cent a telephone. The main difference from the population in general came in car ownership, with 75 per cent of the study families owning at least one car, compared with 60 per cent of families in Britain. The difference probably reflects the fact that the category of 'families in Britain' includes single parent families, who have much lower rates of car ownership, while the study families not only had two parents but also lived in a relatively rural area where car ownership was more necessary. Table A1.6 suggests, however, that in terms of subjective experience of changes in standard of living over the past five years, the study couples differed from the population of Britain as a whole. More of the sample felt that they had grown better off

Table A1.6 *Financial position compared with five years ago*

	This study		Britain 1983*
	Women %	Men %	%
Percentage considering themselves to be:			
better off now	39	40	32
about the same	17	15	27
worse off	44	43	40
don't know	1	2	–

* Jowell and Airey, 1984

in recent years, but equally more felt that they were worse off. This subjective sense of changes in standard of living reflects a more general polarisation in which the rich have got richer and the poor poorer.

Tables A1.1 to A1.6 suggest that there are reasonable similarities between the couples who took part in this study and a wider population of married couples with dependent children. There is therefore some justification for using this study to develop broader generalisations about patterns of allocation of money in Britain.

Appendix 2

The relationship between income and housekeeping money

This analysis was concerned with the relationship between income and the amount spent on housekeeping. The total income of each household was made up of contributions from both wife and husband, coming to them either as wages and salaries or as child benefit or other social security payments. Did the variations in housekeeping money depend in any way on the proportion contributed by each partner?

This question was examined statistically by means of a linear regression analysis. The analysis explored the relationship between, on the one hand, the husband's income, the wife's income and their total joint income and, on the other hand, the amount spent on housekeeping. The first step was to examine the relationship between the husband's income and housekeeping. As might be expected, the regression analysis showed a positive relationship, in that as the husband's income increased the amount spent on housekeeping also increased. The relationship was statistically significant ($r^2 = 0.186$, $t = 4.59$) and could be expressed as an equation:

(a) $HK = £25.49 + 0.1226\ (HI)$
   in which HK = the amount spent on housekeeping
   HI = the husband's income

The analysis showed that if the husband's income rose by one standard deviation (£48) the housekeeping typically rose by £5.88.

The next step was to examine the relationship between the wife's income and the amount spent as housekeeping, that is to say ignoring the contribution made by the husband. Again the regression analysis showed a positive and statistically significant correlation ($r^2 = 0.094$, $t = 3.08$). The more a woman earned the more the household was likely to be spending as housekeeping. Again, this could be expressed as an equation:

(b) $HK = £34.12 + 0.1907\ (W1)$
   in which WI = wife's income

The analysis showed that if the wife's income rose by one standard deviation

(£22) the housekeeping typically rose by £4.14. Notice that these regressions suggest that the constant term (£25.49 in (a) and £34.12 in (b)) may represent in some actuarial sense the average contribution of the other partner.

The third step involved adding together the incomes of husband and wife in order to explore the relationship between the total income and housekeeping. The relationship was again positive, with an increase in its statistical significance ($r^2 = 0.339$, $t = 6.87$). These figures mean that 33.9 per cent of the variation in housekeeping monies could be explained by variations in total household income, 18.6 per cent by variations in the husband's income and 9.4 per cent by variations in the wife's income; these differences are mainly the product of the much larger sums earned by husbands. The relevant equation was:

(c) $HK = £13.90 + 0.1685 \, (TI)$
       in which TI — total income of husband and wife

If the total income rose by one standard deviation (£47) the amount spent on housekeeping typically increased by £7.88.

Finally a multiple regression analysis was used to examine the husband's income, the wife's income and the amount spent on housekeeping together, in order to examine the relative contribution which each income producer made to housekeeping. This analysis showed that 37.8 per cent of the variance in housekeeping could be attributed to variations in the husband and wife's incomes and that the relationship between housekeeping and the two forms of income, taken separately but considered together, was highly significant ($r^2 = 0.378$, $t = 6.45$ and $t = 5.30$). The relationship could be expressed as an equation:

(d) $HK = £11.29 + 0.1573 \, (H1) + 0.2834 \, (W1)$

The coefficients (0.1573 and 0.2834) overlapped in the two standard deviations range, but a t test showed that they were significantly different from each other ($t = 6.57$). The analysis showed that if the husband's income rose by one standard deviation (£48), while the wife's income was held constant, the amount spent on housekeeping would typically rise by £7.50. On the other hand if the husband's income was held constant, while the wife's income rose by one standard deviation (£22), then housekeeping typically rose by £6.16.

In conclusion, this analysis has shown that the amount spent on housekeeping was related both to the level of household income and to the amount contributed by each partner. The regression analysis suggested that

(a) The husband contributed most absolutely to housekeeping since on average his income was four times as great as that of his wife.

(b) The wife contributed most relatively to housekeeping; this meant that if the incomes of wife and husband rose by the same amount 28 per cent of her increase would go to housekeeping compared with 16 per cent of his.

We have seen that the amount spent on housekeeping was likely to differ depending on who earned the money: did it also differ according to who controlled the family's finances? Table A2.1 suggests that the way in which household finances were organised, and the person who controlled the money, had a powerful influence on the housekeeping ratio, that is on the proportion of total income spent as housekeeping. Where wives controlled finances the housekeeping ratio was likely to be higher than in households where husbands controlled finances. Thus at one extreme, in wife-controlled systems, two-thirds of couples spent over a quarter of total household income on housekeeping; at the other extreme, in husband-controlled systems, only two-fifths of couples spent more than a quarter of their total income on housekeeping. This difference was statistically significant.

The same pattern existed for the mean housekeeping ratio, that is for the average proportion of income going to housekeeping. As Table A2.1 shows, the ratio was nearly a third in households where women controlled finances but only one quarter where men were in control. However, some of this difference probably reflected differences in income levels. As we have seen, housekeeping ratios are lower at higher income levels and the table shows mean incomes increasing from £124 per week where wives controlled finances to £173 where husbands were in control. The conclusion of this analysis is that the amount spent on housekeeping is related, first, to the level of household income, secondly, to the sources of that income and thirdly, to the control of income within the household.

Table A2.1 *Housekeeping ratio by control of household finances*

Housekeeping ratio	Wife control N=14	Wife-controlled pooling N=27	Husband-controlled pooling N=36	Husband control N=19
Low	5	9	21	11
High	9	18	15	8
Mean housekeeping ratio	0.32	0.29	0.26	0.26
Standard deviation	±0.16	±0.10	±0.07	±0.13
Mean income £ p w	124	157	165	173
Standard deviation	±40.0	±34.2	±43.4	±61.7

Significance: $p < 0.05$

Key

1 Housekeeping ratio = $\dfrac{\text{Wife's estimate of housekeeping}}{\text{Total household income}}$

2 Low ratio: range = 0.090–0.247
              mean = 0.197

3 High ratio: range = 0.249–0.752
               mean = 0.353

Bibliography

N. W. Alcock (1981) *Warwickshire Grazier and London Skinner 1532–1555, The Account Book of Peter Temple and Thomas Heritage*, London, Oxford University Press.

G. Allan (1985) *Family Life*, Basil Blackwell, Oxford.

M. Anderson (1971) *Family Structure in Nineteenth Century Lancashire*, Cambridge University Press.

P. Ashley (1983) *The Money Problems of the Poor*, Heinemann Educational Books, London.

P. Ayers and J. Lambertz (1986) 'Marriage relations, money and domestic violence in working class Liverpool, 1919–1939', in *Labour and Love*, edited by J. Lewis, Basil Blackwell, Oxford.

S. Baldwin (1985) *The Costs of Caring: Families with Disabled Children*, Routledge and Kegan Paul, London.

J. A. Banks (1954) *Prosperity and Parenthood*, Routledge and Kegan Paul, London.

M. Barrett and M. McIntosh (1980) 'The "family wage": some problems for socialists and feminists', *Capital and Class*, 11, 51–72.

R. D. Baxter (1868) *National Income*, Macmillan, London.

G. S. Becker (1981) *A Treatise on the Family*, Harvard University Press, London.

I. Beeton (1861) *The Book of Household Management*, Beeton, London.

Lady Bell (1911) *At the Works*, Thomas Nelson, London.

C. Bell and H. Roberts (1984) *Social Researching*, Routledge and Kegan Paul, London.

J. Bernard (1972) *The Future of Marriage*, York University Press, New Haven.

V. Binney, G. Harkell and J. Nixon (1981) *Leaving Violent Men: A Study of Refuges and Housing for Battered Women*, Womens Aid Federation, London.

C. Bird (1979) *The Two-Paycheck Marriage*, Pocket Books, New York.

Bird's Eye (1983) *Housekeeping Monitor 1983*, Public Relations Department, Bird's Eye Ltd.

R. L. Blumberg (1988) *Income under Female vs. Male Control: Differential Spending Patterns and the Consequences when Women Lose Control of Returns to Labor*, World Bank Population and Human Resources Series, New York.

P. Blumstein and P. Schwartz (1983) *American Couples*, William Morrow and Company, New York.

L. Bonfield (1979) 'Marriage settlements and the rise of great estates: the demographic aspect', *Economic History Review*, XXXII, 4, 483–493.

L. Bonfield (1983) *Marriage Settlements, 1601–1740: the Adoption of the Strict Settlement*, Cambridge University Press.

C. Booth (1903) *Life and Labour of the People of London*, Macmillan, London.

G. Bourne (1901) *The Bettesworth Book: Talks with a Surrey Peasant*, Larnley and Co, London.

J. Bradshaw and T. Harris (1983) *Energy and Social Policy*, Routledge and Kegan Paul, London.

P. Branca (1976) *Silent Sisterhood: Middle Class Women in the Victorian Home*, Carnegie Mellon, Pittsburgh.

J. Brannen and G. Wilson (1987) *Give and Take in Families: Studies in Resource Distribution*, Allen and Unwin, London.

J. Broad (1979) 'Gentry finances and the Civil War: the case of the Buckinghamshire Verneys', *Economic History Review*, XXXII, 2, 183–200.

J. Brown (1988) *Child Benefit: Investing in the Future*, Child Poverty Action Group, London.

J. Burnett (1974) *Useful Toil*, Allen Lane, London.

C. Callender (1987) 'Redundancy, unemployment and poverty', in *Women and Poverty in Britain*, edited by C. Glendinning and J. Millar, Wheatsheaf Books, Brighton.

A. S. Carloni (1987) *Women in Development*, Agency for International Development, Washington D.C.

Central Statistical Office (1979) *Social Trends, 10*, HMSO, London.

Central Statistical Office (1983) *Social Trends, 14*, HMSO, London.

Central Statistical Office (1986) *Social Trends, 16*, HMSO, London.

Chambers (1952) *Twentieth Century Dictionary*, edited by William Geddie, Chambers, Edinburgh.

Chancellor of the Exchequer (1980) *The Taxation of Husband and Wife*, Cmnd 8093, HMSO, London.

Chancellor of the Exchequer (1986) *The Reform of Personal Taxation*, Cmnd 9756, HMSO, London.

N. Charles and M. Kerr (1987) 'Just the way it is: gender and age differences in family food consumption', in *Give and Take in Families*, edited by J. Brannen and G. Wilson, Allen and Unwin, London.

N. Charles and M. Kerr (1988) *Women, Food and Families*, Manchester University Press.

M. Chaytor (1980) 'Household and Kinship: Ryton in the late 16th and early 17th centuries', *History Workshop Journal*, 10, 25–60.

C. Clay (1968) 'Marriage, inheritance and the use of large estates in England, 1660–1815', *Economic History Review*, XXI, 3, 503–518.

J. S. Cobb and D. P. B. Miles (1983) 'Estimating list inflation in a practice register', *British Medical Journal*, 287, 1434–1436.

L. Comer (1974) *Wedlocked Women*, Feminist Books.

F. A. Cowell (1986) *Micro-economic Principles*, Philip Allan, Oxford.

A. Cragg and T. Dawson (1984) *Unemployed Women: a Study of Attitudes and Experiences*, Department of Employment Research Paper, No. 47, London.

E. M. Craik (1984) *Marriage and Property*, Aberdeen University Press.

R. E. Cromwell and D. Olson (1975) *Power in Families*, Sage Publications, New York.

A. Dale, N. Gilbert and S. Arber (1985) 'Integrating women into class theory', *Sociology*, 19, 3, 384–408.

W. Daniel (1975) *The PEP Survey on Inflation*, XLI, 553, Political and Economic Planning, London.

L. Davidoff and C. Hall (1987) *Family Fortunes*, Hutchinson, London.

L. Davidoff, J. L'Espérance and H. Newby (1976) 'Landscape with figures', in J. Mitchell and A. Oakley (eds.) *The Rights and Wrongs of Women*, Penguin Books, Harmondsworth.

A. Davies (1917) *Autobiography of Thomas Raymond, and Memoirs of the Family of Guise of Elmore*, Camden Society, Gloucestershire.

R. Deem (1986) *All Work and No Play: the Sociology of Women and Leisure*, Open University Press, Milton Keynes.

C. Delphy (1984) *Close to Home*, Hutchinson, London.

N. Dennis, F. Henriques and C. Slaughter (1956) *Coal is Our Life*, Eyre & Spottiswoode, London.

Department of the Environment (1981) *Labour Force Survey*, HMSO, London

Department of Health and Social Security (1977) *Report of the Committee on One-Parent Families* (Finer Report), HMSO, London.

A. V. Dicey (1920) *Lectures on the Relation between Law and Public Opinion in England during the Nineteenth Century*, Macmillan, London.

A. Dilnot (1986) 'Not her own income?' *New Society*, 7 March, 415.

R. E. Dobash and R. P. Dobash (1980) *Violence against Wives*, Open Books, London.

R. E. Dobash and F. Wasoff (1986) *Financial Aspects of Divorce*, research report submitted to the Economic and Social Research Council.

D. Dwyer and J. Bruce (1988) *A Home Divided: Women and Income in the Third World*, Stanford University Press, Palo Alto, C.A.

S. Edgell (1980) *Middle Class Couples*, Allen and Unwin, London.

M. Edwards (1981) *Financial Arrangements within Families*, National Women's Advisory Council, Canberra.

M. Edwards (1981a) 'Financial arrangements within families', *Social Security Journal*, December, 1–16.

M. Edwards (1984) *The Income Unit in the Australian Tax and Social Security Systems*, Institute of Family Studies, Melbourne.

J. Eekelaar (1978) *Family Law and Social Policy*, Weidenfeld and Nicolson, London.

J. Eekelaar and M. MacLean (1986) *Maintenance After Divorce*, Clarendon Press, Oxford.

S. E. Ellis (1846) *The Wives of England*, Griffin, London.

E.T. (1632) *The Lawes Resolutions of Womens Rights: or the Lawes Provision for Women*, Assignes of John More Esq. London.

E. Evason (1982) *Hidden Violence: a Study of Battered Women in Northern Ireland*, Belfast, Farset Press.

Family Finances Group (1983) *Marriages and Money: Forms of Financial Arrangement within the Family*, mimeo, University of Surrey, Department of Sociology.

G. Fiegehen, P. Lansley and A. Smith (1977) *Poverty and Progress in Britain 1953–73*, Cambridge University Press.

Financial Times (1988) 'The taxation of marriage', 19 January.

J. Finch and D. Groves (1983) *A Labour of Love: Women, Work and Caring*, Routledge and Kegan Paul, London.

M. Finer and O. McGregor (1974) The history of the obligation to maintain, in *Report of the Committee on One Parent Families* (the Finer Report), Cmnd 5629-1, HMSO, London.

J. Fitz and J. Hood-Williams (1982) 'The generation game', in *Rethinking Social Inequality*, edited by J. Robbins *et al.*, Gower, Aldershot.

A. Fitzherbert (1534) *The Book of Husbandry*, Thomas Berthelet.

G. Fox (1765) *A Journal*, Richardson and Clark, London.

D. Gillespie (1971) 'Who has the power? The marital struggle', in H. P. Deitzel (ed.) *Marriage and the Struggle of the Sexes*, Collier-Macmillan, New York.

C. Glendinning and J. Millar (1987) *Women and Poverty in Britain*, Wheatsheaf Books, Brighton.

J. Goldthorpe, D. Lockwood, F. Bechofer and J. Platt (1969) *The Affluent Worker in the Class Structure*, Cambridge University Press.

J. Goody (1976) *Production and Reproduction*, Cambridge University Press.

G. Gorer (1971) *Sex and Marriage in England Today*, Nelson, London.

H. Graham (1984) *Women, Health and the Family*, Harvester Press, Brighton.

H. Graham (1985) *Caring for the Family*, The report on a study of the organisation of health resources and responsibilities in 102 families with pre-school children, Open University.

A. Gray (1974) *The Working Class Family as an Economic Unit*, unpublished Ph.D Thesis, Edinburgh University.

A. Gray (1979) 'The working class family as an economic unit', in *The Sociology of the Family*, edited by C. Harris, Sociological Review Monograph, University of Keele.

E. Green, S. Hebron and D. Woodward (1986) *Leisure and Gender, a Study of Sheffield Women's Leisure Experiences*, final report on the project, Sheffield City Polytechnic.

Guardian (1986) 'Till tax do us part', 20 March.

H. J. Habakkuk (1950) 'Marriage settlements in the eighteenth century', *Transactions of the Royal Historical Society*, XXXII.

L. Hamill (1979) *Wives as Sole and Joint Breadwinners*, Government Economic Service Working Paper, No. 15.

M. Henwood and M. Wicks (1986) *Benefit or Burden: the Objectives and Impact of Child Support*, Family Policy Studies Centre, London.

L. Holcombe (1983) *Wives and Property*, Martin Robertson, Oxford.

W. S. Holdsworth (1923–1966) *History of English Law*, 16 vols, Methuen, London.

M. Homer, A. Leonard and P. Taylor (1984) *Private Violence and Public Shame*, Cleveland Refuge and Aid for Women and Children.

M. Homer, A. Leonard and P. Taylor (1985) 'The burden of dependency', in *Marital Violence*, edited by N. Johnson, Routledge and Kegan Paul, London.

R. Hertz (1986) *More Equal than Others: Women and Men in Dual Career Marriages*, University of California Press.

R. A. Houlbrooke (1984) *The English Family 1450–1700*, Longman, London.

C. Howell (1976) 'Peasant inheritance customs in the Midlands, 1280–1700', in *Family and Inheritance*, edited by J. Goody, J. Thirsk and E. P. Thompson, Cambridge University Press.

M. V. Hughes (1946) *A London Family: 1870–1900*, Oxford University Press, London.

S. Hull (1982) *Chaste, Silent and Obedient: English Books for Women: 1475–1640*, San Marino, Huntington Library.

E. H. Hunt (1981) *British Labour History: 1815–1914*, Weidenfeld and Nicolson, London.

P. Hunt (1978) 'Cash transactions and household tasks', *Sociological Review*, 26, 1, 555–571.

P. Hunt (1980) *Gender and Class Consciousness*, Macmillan, London.

J. Jensen (1980) 'Cloth, butter and boarders: women's household production for the market', *Review of Radical Political Economics*, 12, 2.

P. Jephcott, N. Sear and J. Smith (1962) *Married Women Working*, Allen and Unwin, London.

A. John (1982) 'Scratching the surface: Women, work and coalmining in England and Wales', *Oral History*, 10, 2, 13–26.

S. R. Johansson (1977) 'Sex and death in Victorian England: an examination of age and sex-specific death rates, 1840–1910', in *A Widening Sphere*, edited by M. Vicinis, Indiana University Press, Bloomington.

H. G. Jones (1985) 'Consumer behaviour', in *The Economic System in the UK*, edited by D. Morris, Oxford University Press.

H. Joshi (1987) 'The cost of caring', in *Women and Poverty in Britain*, edited by C. Glendinning and J. Millar, Wheatsheaf Books, Brighton.

R. Jowell and C. Airey (1985) *British Social Attitudes: the 1984 Report* Gower, Aldershot.

R. Jowell, S. Witherspoon and L. Brook (1987) *British Social Attitudes: the 1987 Report*, Social and Community Planning Research, London.

O. Kahn-Freund (1971) 'Matrimonial property and equality before the law: some sceptical reflections', *Revue des Droits de l'Homme*, 4, 493–510.

J. Kay (1985) 'Transferable tax allowances', *Fiscal Studies*, 6, 2, 67–70.

J. Kay and C. Sandler (1982) 'The taxation of husband and wife: a view of the debate in the Green Paper', *Fiscal Studies*, 3, 3, 173–185

W. Kemsley, R. Redpath and M. Holmes (1980) *Family Expenditure Survey Handbook*, HMSO, London.

M. Kerr (1958) *The People of Ship Street*, Routledge and Kegan Paul, London.

M. Kerr and N. Charles (1986) 'Servers and providers: the distribution of food within the family', *Sociological Review*, 34, 1, 115–157.

J. Klein (1965) *Samples from English Cultures*, Routledge and Kegan Paul, London.

M. W. Labarge (1980) *A Baronial Household of the Thirteenth Century*, Harvester Press, Brighton.

H. Land (1969) *Large Families in London*, Bell, London.

H. Land (1975) 'The introduction of family allowances', in *Change, Choice and Conflict in Social Policy*, edited by P. Hall, H. Land, R. Parker and A. Webb, Heinemann, London.

H. Land (1977) 'Inequalities in large families: more of the same or different?' in *Equalities and Inequalities in Family Life*, edited by R. Chester and J. Peel, Academic Press, London.

H. Land (1980) 'The family wage', *Feminist Review*, 6, 55–77.

H. Land (1983) 'Poverty and gender: the distribution of resources within the family', in *The Structure of Disadvantage*, edited by M. Brown, Heinemann, London.

H. Land (1986) 'Women and children last: reform of social security', in *The Yearbook of Social Policy in Britain, 1985–6*, edited by M. Brenton and C. Ungerson, Routledge and Kegan Paul, London.

Law Commission (1985) *Transfer of Money between Spouses – the Married Women's Property Act 1964*, Working Paper No. 90, HMSO, London.

L. Lawner (1973) *Letters from Prison by Antonio Gramsci*, Harper and Row, New York.

G. G. Leaver (1987) 'Getting by without employment', in *Redundancy and Recession*, edited by C. Harris, Basil Blackwell, Oxford.

L. Leghorn and K. Parker (1981) *Woman's Worth: Sexual Economics and the World of Women*, Routledge and Kegan Paul, London.

D. Leonard (1980) *Sex and Generation*, Tavistock, London.

F. Le Play (1855) *Les Ouvriers Europeens*, L'imprimerie impériale, Paris.

J. Lewis and D. Piachaud (1987) 'Women and poverty in the twentieth century', in *Women and Poverty in Britain*, edited by C. Glendinning and J. Millar, Wheatsheaf Books, Brighton.

M. Llewelyn Davies (1915) *Maternity: Letters from Working Women*, G. Bell and Sons, London.

M. Loane (1905) *The Queen's Poor*, Edward Arnold, London.

M. Loane (1909) *An Englishman's Castle*, Edward Arnold, London.

E. C. Lodge (1927) *The Account Book of a Kentish Estate 1616–1704*, Oxford University Press, London.

S. Lukes (1974) *Power: a Radical View*, Macmillan, London.

R. W. Malcolmson (1981) *Life and Labour in England: 1700–1780*, Hutchinson, London.

A. Marsh (1978) *Women and Shiftwork*, HMSO, London.

J. Martin and C. Roberts (1984) *Women and Employment: a Lifetime Perspective*, HMSO, London.

G. W. McDonald (1980) 'Family power: the assessment of a decade of theory and research, 1970–1979', *Journal of Marriage and the Family*, 841–854.

K. D. MacLeod (1977) *The Family Economy and the Standard of Living*, Report to the Joseph Rowntree Memorial Trust.

S. McRae (1987) 'The allocation of money in cross-class families', *Sociological Review*, 35, 1, 97–122.

S. Meacham (1977) *A Life Apart*, Thames and Hudson, London.

J. S. Mill (1869) *The Subjection of Women*, Oxford University Press, London.

J. Millar (1987) 'The costs of marital breakdown', in *Money Matters*, edited by R. Walker and G. Parker, Sage Publications, London.

N. Millward (1968) 'Family status and behaviour at work', *Sociological Review*, 16, 2, 149–164.

M. Mitterauer and R. Sieder (1982) *The European Family*, Basil Blackwell, Oxford.

D. H. J. Morgan (1985) *The Family, Politics and Social Theory*, Routledge and Kegan Paul, London.

L. Morris (1984) 'Redundancy and patterns of household finance', *Sociological Review*, 33, 3, 492–523.

L. Morris (1987) 'Constraints on gender: the family wage, social security and the labour market', *Work, Employment and Society*, 1, 1, 85–106.

L. Morris and S. Ruane (1986) *Household Finances Management and Labour Market Behaviour*, Work and Employment Research Unit, University of Durham.

K. Mourby (1983) 'The wives and children of the Teeside unemployed 1919–1939', *Oral History*, 11, 2, 56–60.

A. Murcott (1982) ' "Its a pleasure to cook for him": food, meal times and gender in some South Wales households', in *The Public and the Private*, edited by E. Garmarnikow, D. Morgan, J. Purvis and D. Taylorson, Heinemann, London.

National Consumer Council (1975) *For Richer, for Poorer*, London.

J. Nelson (1983) 'What it costs – and where it goes', *Woman's Realm*, March, 27–30.

A. Oakley (1974) *The Sociology of Housework*, Martin Robertson, Oxford.

D. J. Oddy (1970) 'Working class diets in nineteenth century Britain', *Economic History Review*, XVIII, 314–323.

Office of Population Censuses and Surveys (1970) *Classification of Occupations*, HMSO, London.

Office of Population Censuses and Surveys (1984) *General Household Survey 1983*, HMSO, London.

Office of Population Censuses and Surveys (1985) *Family Expenditure Survey*, HMSO, London.

T. Oliver (1895) 'The diet of toil', *Lancet*, 29 June, 1629–35.

K. O'Donovan (1985) *Sexual Divisions in Law*, Weidenfeld and Nicolson, London.

L. Oren (1974) 'The welfare of women in labouring families: England, 1860–1950', in *Clio's Consciousness Raised*, edited by M. Hartman and L. Banner, Harper and Row, New York.

J. Pahl (1980) 'Patterns of money management within marriage', *Journal of Social Policy*, 9, 3, 313–335.

J. Pahl (1983) 'The allocation of money and the structuring of inequality within marriage', *Sociological Review*, 13, 2, 237–262.

J. Pahl (1984) 'The allocation of money within the household', in *The State, The Law and the Family*, edited by M. Freeman, Tavistock, London.

J. Pahl (1985) *Private Violence and Public Policy*, Routledge and Kegan Paul, London.

J. Pahl (1985a) 'Who benefits from child benefit?', *New Society*, 25 April, 117–119.

J. Pahl (1986) 'Expenditure and the family', in *America in Perspective*, edited by Oxford Analytica, Houghton Mifflin Company, Boston.

R. E. Pahl (1984) *Divisions of Labour*, Basil Blackwell, Oxford

G. Parker (1987) 'Fuel poverty', in *Money Matters*, edited by G. Parker and R. Walker, Sage, London.

M. Pember Reeves (1914) *Round About a Pound a Week*, G. Bell and Sons, London.

M. Pennington (1848) *A Brief Account of my Exercises from my Childhood*, Philadelphia.

N. Penney (1920) *The Household Account Book of Sarah Fell of Swathmore Hall*, Cambridge University Press.

D. Piachaud (1982) 'Patterns of Income and Expenditure within Families', *Journal of Social Policy*, 11, 4, 469–482.

J. Platt (1987) 'Research dissemination: a case study', *The Quarterly Journal of Social Affairs*, 3, 3, 181–198.

H. Qureshi and K. Simons (1987) 'Resources within families: caring for elderly people', in *Give and Take in Families*, edited by J. Brannen and G. Wilson, Allen and Unwin, London.

R. Rapoport and R. Rapoport (1975) *Leisure and the Family Life Cycle*, Routledge and Kegan Paul, London.

E. Rathbone (1924) *The Disinherited Family*, Edward Arnold, London.

E. Roberts (1977) 'Working class women in the North West', *Oral History*, 5, 2, 7–30.

E. Roberts (1984) *A Woman's Place*, Basil Blackwell, Oxford.

H. Roberts (1981) *Doing Feminist Research*, Routledge and Kegan Paul, London.

T. Robinson (1788) *The Common Law of Kent, or the Customs of Gavelkind*, P. Uriel, London.

B. Rogers (1980) *The Domestication of Women*, Tavistock Publications, London.

B. Rogers (1984) *Intrahousehold Allocation of Resources and Roles: an Annotated Bibliography of the Methodological and Empirical Literature*, Bureau for Program and Policy Coordination, Agency for International Development, Washington D.C.

E. Ross (1982) 'Survival networks: women's neighbourhood sharing in London before World War I', *History Workshop Journal*, 13, 4–27.

B. S. Rowntree (1901) *Poverty: A Study of Town Life*, Macmillan, London.

C. Safilios Rothschild (1969) 'Family sociology or wives' family sociology?', *Journal of Marriage and the Family*, 31, 290–301.

C. Safilios Rothschild (1970) 'The study of family power structure: a review 1960–1969', *Journal of Marriage and the Family*, 32 (November), 539–552.

J. Scanzoni (1979) 'Social processes and power in families' in *Contemporary Theories about the Family*, edited by W. Burr, R. Hill, I. Nye and I. Reiss, The Free Press, New York.

H. Scott (1984) *Working Your Way to the Bottom: the Feminisation of Poverty*, Pandora Press, London.

Secretary of State for the Environment (1986) *Paying for Local Government*, Cmnd 9714, HMSO, London.

S. Shimmin (1962) 'Extra-mural factors influencing behaviour at work', *Occupational Psychology*, 36, 2, 124–36.

T. Smith (1583) *De Republica Anglomon: The Maner of Gouvernement or Policie of the Realme of England*, H. Midleton, London.

P. Stamp (1985) 'Balance of financial power in marriage', *Sociological Review*, 33, 3, 546–66.

P. Stearns (1972) 'Working class-women in Britain, 1890–1914', in *Suffer and Be Still*, edited by M. Vicinus, Methuen, London.

E. Symons and I. Walker (1986) 'The reform of personal taxation: a brief analysis', *Fiscal Studies*, 7, 2, 38–47.

L. Syson and M. Young (1974) 'Poverty in Bethnal Green', in M. Young (ed.) *Poverty Report 1974*, Temple Smith.

M. Talbot (1982) *Women and Leisure: a State of the Art Review*, Social Science Research Council/Sports Council, London.

S. Taylor (1977) 'The effect of marriage on job possibilities for women and the ideology of the home', *Oral History*, 5, 2, 46–59.

P. Thane (1978) 'Women and the Poor Law in Victorian and Edwardian England', *History Workshop Journal*, 6, 29–51.

G. Therborn (1980) *The Ideology of Power and the Power of Ideology*, New Left Books, London.

E. P. Thompson (1976) 'The grid of inheritance', in *Family and Inheritance: Rural Society in Western Europe, 1200–1800*, edited by J. Goody, J. Thirsk and E. P. Thompson, Cambridge University Press.

F. Thompson (1945) *Lark Rise to Candleford*, Oxford University Press, London.

Times, The (1985) 'His and her income' and 'Tax change for couples condemned by peers', 11 December.

J. E. Todd and L. M. Jones (1972) *Matrimonial Property*, HMSO, London.

P. Townsend (1979) *Poverty in the United Kingdom*, Penguin, Harmondsworth.

J. Treble (1979) *Urban Poverty in Britain*, Batsford, London.

H. T. Turner (1841) *Manners and Household Expenses of the Thirteenth and Fifteenth Centuries*, William Nicol, Shakespeare Press, London.

T. Tusser (1562) *A Hundreth Good Pointes of Husbandrie*, Richard Totelli, London.

C. Ungerson (1987) *Policy is Personal: Sex, Gender and Informal Care*, Tavistock, London.

R. T. Vann (1979) 'Wills and the family in an English town: Banbury, 1550–1800', *Journal of Family History*, 4, 4, 346–367.

D. Vincent (1981) *Bread, Knowledge and Freedom*, Methuen, London.

R. Walker and G. Parker (1987) *Money Matters: Income, Wealth and Financial Welfare*, Sage Publications, London.

J. Walsh (1857) *A Manual of Domestic Economy: Suited to Families Spending from £100 to £1000 a Year*, Routledge and Kegan Paul, London.

A. Walsh and R. Lister (1985) *Mother's Life-line: a Survey of How Women Use and Value Child Benefit*, Child Poverty Action Group, London.

E. Warren (1864) *How I Managed my House on Two Hundred Pounds a Year*, Houlston, London.

L. Weitzman (1985) *The Divorce Revolution*, The Free Press, New York.

A. Whitehead (1981) ' "I'm hungry mum": the politics of domestic budgeting', in *Of Marriage and the Market*, edited by K. Young, C. Wolkowitz and R. McCullagh, CSE Books, London.

K. Whitehorn (1982) 'What's mine's yours', *Observer*, 28 February.

G. Wilson (1987) *Money in the Family*, Avebury, Aldershot.

G. Wilson (1987a) 'Money: patterns of responsibility and irresponsibility', in *Give and Take in Families*, edited by J. Brannen and G. Wilson, Allen and Unwin, London.

A. S. Wohl (1978) *The Victorian Family*, Croom Helm, London.

K. Wrightson (1982) *English Society: 1580–1680*, Hutchinson, London.

M. Young (1952) 'Distribution of income within the family', *British Journal of Sociology*, 3, 305–321.

M. Young (1977) 'Housekeeping money', in *Why the Poor Pay More*, edited by F. Williams, Macmillan, London.

M. Young and P. Willmott (1973) *The Symmetrical Family*, Routledge and Kegan Paul, London.

F. Zweig (1961) *The Worker in an Affluent Society*, Heinemann Educational Books, London.

Index